# The Greatest Masters

NOVELS BY STEPHEN GOODWIN

*Kin*
*The Blood of Paradise*

# The Greatest Masters

## The 1986 Masters & Golf's Elite

**STEPHEN GOODWIN**

*1817*

**HARPER & ROW, PUBLISHERS, New York**
Cambridge, Philadelphia, San Francisco, Washington
London, Mexico City, São Paulo, Singapore, Sydney

FIRST EDITION

*Copyeditor: Jean Touroff*

*Designer: Helene Berinsky*

---

Library of Congress Cataloging-in-Publication Data
Goodwin, Stephen.
  The greatest Masters.
  1. Masters Golf Tournament.   I. Title.
GV970.G66   1988        796.352′74        87-45621
ISBN 0-06-015874-3

---

88 89 90 91 92 HC 10 9 8 7 6 5 4 3 2 1

*To all those who have been such good
and true companions
from the first hole to the last*

# Contents

*Photos follow page 80.*

# Preface and Acknowledgments

Any writer who attempts to reconstruct a golf tournament has to rely on the help and eyewitness testimony of a great many people. The action of a tournament is spread out over a couple hundred acres, and at any given moment there are so many skirmishes, retreats, and advances taking place that no one can possibly see every shot that affects the outcome. It's simply not possible to always be in the right place at the right time—and even when you are, you share the view with a thousand other fans who are straining just as hard to see the club flash and the ball fly.

So I talked to as many people as I could who had something to say about the winning and losing of the 1986 Masters. I talked to players, caddies, photographers, other golf writers, and scores of ordinary fans. (Though the people who travel to Augusta year after year are anything but ordinary, they know the course inside out, and they know their golf.) My task was made easier, of course, by the fact that millions of words were written about the tournament and that so many hours of play were televised. Anne Luzzato, formerly of CBS, and Bonnie Lyster, of USA Network, were kind enough to make complete tapes available to me.

I pored over them for days, though the tapes don't tell anything like the whole story—at least not the story I wanted to tell. Careers were on the line at Augusta, and the most

talented golfers in the game—the golfers who battled to win
the fiftieth Masters—brought with them long and complicated
histories, not to mention profoundly different approaches to
the game. If you believe, as I do, that a round of golf speaks
volumes about a man's character, then you want to see more
of his round than a few select shots.

Championship golf tests an athlete's mental and emotional stamina like no other sport. The player in contention has
to maintain not only the rhythm and tempo of his swing, which
is difficult enough, but something far more elusive—his confidence. There is no flow of the game except the flow he creates;
there's no clock ticking away, no teammate to pick up the
slack, nothing at all to respond to—no pitch speeding toward
the plate, no serve curving over the net—except the small
white ball sitting still. As the old saying has it, the golfer is alone
with his God and his shot. To win a championship, the golfer
has to find a way to generate his own confidence, and to keep
it keen and running high, without any letup, for four days and
270-plus shots. This is not an easy task, and one premise of this
book is that every move a golfer makes on the course is designed to contribute to that overriding effort.

Another old saying tells us that golf is two minutes of
action crammed into four hours—but for the golfer, and the
golf fan, drama and tension are built into every second of a
round. I've tried to capture some of those individual dramas,
and as for the larger drama of the tournament itself—well, the
fiftieth Masters was one of those sports events that passes directly into the realm of legend, and it would take the golfing
equivalent of Homer to celebrate it properly. Jack Nicklaus's
victory—his twentieth major championship—was fashioned by
so many magnificent golf shots that, for this writer, the best
seemed to be merely to describe them and let the reader shake
his head in wonder. What made Nicklaus's triumph reverber-
ate was not just his defiance of the odds and the years; his
amazing performance, for a long and lingering moment,
seemed to restore a familiar order to a sport in which the
rumblings of change had grown loud and ominous. The 1986

Masters was a landmark tournament, and it illuminated those changes with unusual clarity.

Among the many who helped me, I want to express special thanks to Nick Price; like all top players, he is regularly pressed for interviews, but he patiently recalled his role in the 1986 Masters and provided many insights that could only have come from a contestant. His caddy, David MacNeilly, has a wealth of shrewd observations about championship golf and the gift of gab to go with them. George Peper and Robin McMillan, both of *Golf* magazine and both close students of the game, helped me put the tournament in a larger perspective. To Nuria Pastor and Dudley Doust I owe much of what I know about European golf and European golfers.

Over the long haul of this book, I talked the ear off my friend and frequent playing partner, Rick Walter. A fine golfer and golf writer, now an editor at the *Los Angeles Times,* he was my sounding board whenever I needed one—which was often. His good judgment and knowledge of the game helped more than he knows.

# The Greatest Masters

# 1

# Slouching Toward Augusta

In golf, the championship season begins with the playing of the Masters. The tournament takes place in the early spring, over the first full weekend in April, in Augusta, Georgia. The time and place have been fixed on every golfer's calendar ever since 1934, when Robert Tyre Jones, Jr., having retired from competitive golf, decided to host a spring get-together. His plans were modest enough, but no event associated with Jones—he was, after all, the immortal Bobby, the man who carried off the Grand Slam in 1930—could remain modest for very long. That first year the tournament went by a simple descriptive name, the Augusta National Invitation Tournament; Jones balked at calling it the Masters, a title that seemed too grandiose. Strictly speaking, it was nothing more than the championship of the Augusta National Golf Club.

Yet the tournament quickly acquired a character and prestige all its own, in large part because Bobby Jones presided over it. Only twenty-nine when he retired, and a living legend if ever there was one, he made an exception for his own tournament and played in every Masters until 1948, never finishing better than 13th. His presence guaranteed a large gallery—the Masters was the only place golf fans could see him in action—and a field made up of the best players in the world. The sporting press, led by Grantland Rice, embraced the Masters; and the tournament chairman, Cliff Roberts, saw to it that the Masters established and maintained a reputation as the best-run event in golf. To receive an invitation to the Masters was, and still is, an honor in itself, and the roster of winners soon became a litany of the truly great golfers of the modern era. The symbol of victory was a green jacket, presented by the defending champion to the new champion, and Jones himself interviewed the winner in a ceremony that captured the imagination of the public, connecting the present with the illustrious past. In his own day, Jones had so thoroughly dominated the golfing world that he was known as Emperor Jones, and at the presentation of the jacket he still seemed to be the spiritual ruler of a peaceful and well-ordered kingdom, conferring a sort of knighthood upon the worthiest young players in the game where he had once reigned supreme.

Nobody can say for sure when the Masters came to be regarded as a major championship. The Grand Slam that Jones completed as an amateur was made up of four national championships—the United States and British Opens, and the United States and British Amateurs. In 1953, when Ben Hogan won the Masters, the U.S. Open, and the British Open, he started people thinking of a professional Grand Slam, and by a kind of popular acclamation, the Masters, along with the Professional Golfers Association Championship, came to rank along with the two national Opens as one of golf's premier events.

By far the youngest of the majors, the Masters had already established its own traditions. For one thing, it was the only one of the four major championships decided in four days of medal play (the PGA was a match-play event, and in the British and U.S. Opens, it was still the custom to play 36 holes on the third and last day of the tournament). The Masters was also unique among the major championships in that it was always played over the same course, and the feats of one champion could readily be compared to those of his predecessors. The Augusta National golf course, designed by Jones in collaboration with Alister Mackenzie, had proved itself to be a true championship layout, one that regularly inspired sensational golf shots and could almost be counted upon to produce a thrilling finish. The tournament was played at a glorious time of year, early April, when the dogwoods, redbuds, azaleas, and other flowering plants were in bloom. Every hole was named for the plant or tree that lined its fairways, and every year the golf-writing press outdid itself in extolling the beauty of the course.

After 1956, when the Masters was first televised, everyone—every American, at least—who followed top-level golf came to know Augusta National as well as or better than any other tournament course in the world. It was every bit as beautiful as the writers had claimed, and people who had never set foot on it knew the key holes by heart. St. Andrew's, in Scotland, would always be the most hallowed of courses, but Augusta National could claim to be its American counterpart. The course and the tournament loomed like some shining vision of Camelot, a vision of grandeur and perfection in a game that, at the professional level, was still young, changing, and far from perfect. Other tournaments came and went, but the Masters never lost its aura of continuity and permanence. Those lucky enough to get badges to the Masters—they were among the most sought-after tickets in sports—set out for Augusta in the spirit of pilgrims returning to a shrine. Old Masters hands could remember a time when the tournament was more intimate, but it still captured both the essence of golf and the essence of spring. In April, when lovers want to go to Paris, golfers everywhere hear the call of the Masters.

In the months preceding the 1986 Masters, the usually bright anticipation was clouded a little. In the kingdom of golf there was unrest, and as the season opened, the man who would be king, Severiano Ballesteros of Spain, was in a strange state of semiexile. A two-time winner of the Masters, Ballesteros had been suspended from the American PGA Tour, although he was still eligible to play in the Masters, a "nontour event" that makes its own rules. The suspension had commanded the attention of the press throughout the winter; and since Ballesteros was one of the favorites to win the tournament, and since he let everyone know exactly what he thought of the suspension ("Who is it good for? Is it good for golf? No! It is good for nobody!"), this particular Masters, the Fiftieth Masters, loomed more and more as a sort of grudge match.

Even though he was a veteran world traveler and the winner of forty-four tournaments around the globe, Ballesteros had yet to shed his reputation as golf's enfant terrible. An emotional player, blessed with huge talent and the dark, fiery good looks of the hero of a romantic novel, he had been all-conquering in Europe, where he enjoyed the status and privileges of a superstar. In the United States, though, Ballesteros had never quite lived up to the high expectations his foreign triumphs had created. True, he had played irregularly in America, but he had only five victories to his credit. Two of those, of course, had come at Augusta, and he had also won two British Opens—a total of four majors, which, for almost any other golfer, would be counted as a remarkable success. Perhaps because Ballesteros had won his first major titles so early and with such apparent ease—he was only twenty-two when he won the 1979 British Open, and the next spring, when he won his first Masters, he had built up a 10-stroke lead with nine holes to play—a strange air of smoldering disappointment hung over his career. It was almost as if he expected other championships to be his for the taking, and couldn't keep himself from sulking when they were not. In any case, Ballesteros had established himself as a once-in-a-generation golfer, one whose place in the history of the game was assured.

And so, when he arrived in Lake City, Florida, to play in the Florida Cup Classic, it was as if Pavarotti had turned up to sing with the local barbershop quartet. The other 256 contestants, most of them armed only with a stubborn dream and a set of clubs, which they carried themselves, had ponied up $500 apiece to play for a share of the $135,000 pot. Ballesteros had been lured to Lake City by a pair of first-class air tickets for him and his caddy and by the opportunity to hone his skills in competition before moving on to Augusta. A golfer has to play somewhere, against somebody, and the Florida Cup Classic, sponsored by the Tournament Players Association, was the only game Ballesteros could find.

In Lake City, Ballesteros made a few tart remarks about Deane Beman, the PGA Tour commissioner. "Deane is one-up on me now," he said, hinting at a personal vendetta, even though the decision to suspend his playing privileges had been made by the tour's ten-member policy board. Briefly, the dispute turned on the fact that during the 1985 season Ballesteros had appeared in only nine tour events instead of the mandatory fifteen. When Beman enforced the decision, he claimed that Ballesteros himself had suggested fifteen as the number of tournaments he could play in the United States and still meet his foreign commitments. Ballesteros denied setting any figure.

The controversy was simple enough on the surface, but everyone who knew anything at all about either Ballesteros or Beman knew that this was a power struggle with ramifications that were anything but simple. Those who sided with Ballesteros argued that even if he had violated the letter of the law, the spirit was in his favor. If the aim of the PGA Tour was to stage the best possible tournaments, with the strongest possible fields, then Ballesteros should play. Both Jack Nicklaus and Tom Watson, in Miami for the Doral Open while Ballesteros was in Lake City, suggested a back-door solution—sponsors' exemptions. All tournament sponsors have a limited number of exemptions, or invitations, that they can issue, and they could approach Ballesteros directly. No dice. The suspension was to be enforced absolutely, and in some quarters it still seemed too lenient. Why, the argument against Ballesteros ran, should he come over here whenever he pleases, and skim the pot? The rule requiring all touring pros to put in a minimum number of appearances had been adopted to prevent exactly that and to make sure that the top players didn't show up only for the choice tournaments. Ballesteros had to pay his dues like everyone else. His critics, pointing out that he received appearance fees in Europe, put him down as a mercenary and charged that he expected preferential treatment. Beman was closemouthed about the matter, but the Spaniard was characteristically outspoken. "Deane Beman," he said, "is a little man trying to be a big man."

He also, uncharacteristically, predicted that he would win both the Masters and the U.S. Open, even though his performance in Lake City hardly seemed to warrant such a bold claim. He played fuzzy golf, winding up with scores of 70–70–73— 213, only three under par, and tied for 22d. His winnings were $1,375.

Ballesteros's schedule called for him to play two other TPA tournaments, but he curtailed it to return to Spain where his father, Baldomero, was suffering from cancer. Seve, the youngest of four sons—all four of them professional golfers— still lived with his parents in Pedrena, the Atlantic coastal village where he was born. Baldomero was the patriarch of the proud, clannish family; in his youth he had been a distance runner and an oarsman in the traditional regattas in nearby Santander, and his death, in late March, came much more swiftly than expected. Ballesteros never spoke publicly about what the loss meant to him, but it added a somber dimension to his preparations for the tournament. Golf fans everywhere understood that the proud, passionate Ballesteros would have a deeper incentive than ever to win at Augusta.

The friction between Ballesteros and the powers-that-be in American golf was nothing new. Since his first visit to this country as a homesick teenager, he'd had reservations about playing here, despite his ambition to be the greatest golfer in the world—*el major golfista del mundo*—and despite his understanding that in order to be recognized as the greatest, he would have to prevail against the Americans. The American PGA Tour was the big leagues, and the European tour was the minors—the best of the minors, but still the minors. Nevertheless, Ballesteros cast his lot in Europe, where he felt at home, and whenever he played against Americans, he played with a particular vengeance. What seemed to goad him on was the assumption that any European who competed against American golfers was automatically an underdog, and any victory by a European a fluky upset. "The Americans are not the best golfers in the world," he often said, and at times he seemed bent on proving his point single-handedly.

When the Ryder Cup matches were played in September 1985 at the Belfry Golf Club in Coldfield, England, Ballesteros had help. He was the catalyst and spiritual leader of the European team—"General Ballesteros," one British writer called him—but the other players were equally determined to make sure that the Ryder Cup remained on their side of the water. This competition between American and British professional golfers was first held in 1927, and the Ryder Cup had been in American hands for so long that, like the America's Cup in sailing, it had almost come to be regarded as a permanent national possession. True, the British had won the Ryder Cup on their home turf in 1957, and in 1969 had eked out a tie; but otherwise the American team had enjoyed fifty years of uninterrupted success. To bolster the British team, the eligibility rules had been changed in 1979 to make room for the talented new players from other European countries. The new European team gave the Americans a scare in 1983, and at the Belfry they were on the verge of winning.

The Europeans were one point ahead after the foursomes and the four-ball matches. This meant that the third and last day, the day of singles competition, would be decisive. The galleries had been large and boisterous throughout the matches, and as the result began to take shape—"the result everyone in Britain had dreamed about," according to one British journalist—they abandoned the traditional standards of decorum. In golf it is etiquette to root *for* someone, never *against,* but these galleries jeered and heckled the Americans and generally let their elation run away with them. In a word, they rubbed it in. The Europeans won seven of the twelve singles matches, and halved another, giving them a comfortable margin of victory, 16½ to 11½. While they were toasting each other with champagne, the Americans were eating humble pie, and they didn't like it, not one bit.

The loss of the Ryder Cup capped a long, awkward season in American golf, a season that began with a European victory in the Masters. This time the winner was Bernhard Langer, the methodical West German with Popeye forearms and Fauntleroy curls. (Although well known to the European golfing public, where he had emerged as Ballesteros's chief rival, he was still so much a stranger in the United States that Masters officials had to ask how to pronounce his name.) Another foreign player, Taiwan's T. C. Chen, was leading the U.S. Open for the first three rounds and into the fourth, when he played a disastrous "double-chip," hitting the ball twice when he tried to lift it from heavy rough. He eventually finished in a tie for second, behind an unlikely American winner, Andy North, but the other runners-up were Dave Barr, a Canadian, and Denis Watson, of Zimbabwe. Still later that summer, a Scotsman, Sandy Lyle, won the British Open, a tournament that Americans had more or less annexed since Arnold Palmer established a winning tradition in 1961. Lyle was the first Briton to win since Tony Jacklin—the captain of the victorious Ryder Cup team—in 1969. Two American veterans, Lee Trevino and Hubert Green, battled it out for the PGA Championship, but their seniority only underscored the point that in the big events, the young American players simply weren't coming through.

Professional golf had taken on a new international flavor, and collectively, the talented players from other countries were billed as the "foreign invasion." Military metaphors have always had a place in the language of golf, but the last person to speak of an invasion was that most magisterial of golf writers, Bernard Darwin, and the invasion that concerned him was the American invasion of Great Britain in the 1920s. Since then American golfers had held more or less uncontested sway over the rest of the golfing world, and the sudden blooming of so many gifted young players from so many foreign lands was frankly disturbing. Were the Ballesteroses, the Langers, and the Lyles the wave of the future? Could it be that golf would go the way of tennis, where foreign players had become dominant? Most worrisome of all, what had happened to a whole generation of American players?

Nobody had much good to say about the most recent crop of golfers on the American tour. They seemed more or less interchangeable, and while any one of them was capable of winning a tournament, none of them seemed to be capable of winning more than once. Over the last two years, there had been seventeen first-time winners on the tour, and their names evoked the barest flicker of recognition. "Who Are These Guys, Anyway?" asked a headline in *Sports Illustrated* a few weeks before the Masters, and the writer, Rick Reilly, answered his own question by describing the new breed of pros as "a decade of floppy disc printouts . . . tan accountants with a lot of pastel shirts." Which was charitable compared to the standard descriptive terms, "drones," "clones," and "robots."

The American PGA Tour was struggling through an identity crisis, and the man called upon to explain it—the man who was sometimes blamed for it—was Deane Beman, the commissioner. A man of Napoleonic stature and determination, he came to the job after a successful playing career that included an Amateur Championship and a second-place finish in the 1969 U.S. Open. Judged strictly by the bottom line, Beman was the best thing that had ever happened to professional golf; he'd ushered the game into a new era of prosperity. When he took over as commissioner in 1974, purses totaled just over $8 million. In 1986, the pros would compete for more than $30 million.

Yet Beman had his critics, among them some of the leading players in the game. The knock on the commissioner was that he had turned the kingdom of golf into a corporation. Not only did tournaments have an ever-changing array of corporate sponsors, but the PGA Tour had a host of official suppliers whose products were relentlessly merchandised. Ben Crenshaw was only one of many golfers who believed that the marketing of the PGA Tour had gone far enough—"We're jamming it down the fans' throats," he said—and he was present at the 1983 showdown at the Westchester Country Club, where a group of pros called Beman on the carpet to account for the way he was managing the tour's affairs.

Beman weathered that storm and moved right along. One of his pet projects was the construction of the new "stadium" courses, designed to accommodate the huge galleries that now could be counted on to show up for tournaments. Also called Tournament Players Courses, they were replacing the more venerable courses traditionally used as tournament sites. Players like Crenshaw and Tom Kite complained that these stadium courses all looked alike, and Tom Watson said flatly, "I'm sick of them." Beman defended the courses on the grounds that they gave more spectators a better view of the action; he might have added that they were also immensely profitable. The symbol of these new courses became the railroad ties used to give a sharp edge to the water hazards, and the standing joke was that one of them would be the first golf course ever to burn down.

But the most serious charge of all was that the tour, with all of Beman's innovations, was producing a generation of mediocre golfers. The members of the Big Three, the heroes of an earlier generation, Gary Player, Arnold Palmer, and Jack Nicklaus, all singled out the establishment of the "all-exempt" tour as the moment Beman chose the primrose path to complacency. Before 1983, only the top 60 players could be assured of tournament berths, and the others had to go through the rigors of weekly qualifying. Now the top 125 players had a free pass, and they were competing for such huge pots of money that they didn't have to win in order to make a good living. One victory every few years, together with a few finishes in the top 10, and a pro could make a very handsome living. On the tour—"out here," as the pros say—tournament sponsors seemed to compete with each other to offer ever-fatter purses, and various corporations put up the money for a whole array of gimmicky point systems and subsidiary competitions (none of them very well understood by the fans, but worth plenty to the players). In short, the PGA Tour provided the spectacle of increasingly anonymous golfers competing for increasingly large sums of money. The tour seemed more and more to be composed of players who lacked the drive to excel of a Palmer, a Player, or—to put it in the terms that really hurt—a Ballesteros.

The younger players on the tour, of course, resented the accusation that they were any less dedicated or talented than their predecessors, or than the foreigners who had come to prominence. They claimed that there were more good players than ever and, consequently, that no one could expect to reel off a string of victories. Still, golf was in the novel situation of having a commissioner who was far better known than most of the players. Beman prided himself on having built golf into a major sport—but it was a major sport with an alarming shortage of stars.

With all the new faces, and new courses, and new names for old tournaments, the game seemed to need personalities; and at least one relatively new American player, Mac O'Grady, was ready to fill the gap. Notorious for his seventeen attempts to pass the tour's Qualifying School, his left-handed putting, and his sesquipedalian language, O'Grady was in the news again at the beginning of the 1986 season for his hostility toward Deane Beman, who had fined him $5,000 and suspended him for six weeks for "conduct unbecoming a professional golfer." The case began in 1984, when O'Grady insulted a volunteer at a tournament, and Beman withheld $500 from his paycheck. Ever after, O'Grady had been on the warpath, and as the Masters approached, he was threatening to file suit against Beman and seek punitive damages amounting to $12 million.

The whole episode was so overblown that at first, against the background of the larger shifts and dislocations in the game, it provided a measure of comic relief. As it dragged on and O'Grady's attacks became more shrill and vituperative— he was publicly comparing Beman to Hitler—the affair curdled and turned into an embarrassment. Professional golf had always been blessedly free of the contention that has become so much a part of other big-money sports, but now, as Tom Watson said, "It's getting to be like baseball, football, and basketball out here. Nothing but controversies."

Running through all these concerns—the suspensions, the politics, the finances, the disappointing performance of American golfers—was the thread of nostalgia. Nowhere is it written that golf must have a king, as opposed to a commissioner, but most golf fans had grown up at a time when there was a ruling dynasty, and one player set a high standard of excellence by which all the rest could be measured. In his time, Bobby Jones was the standard, and he was followed by Ben Hogan and Arnold Palmer; but the age of Jack Nicklaus had lasted longest and, in retrospect, seemed to give off the glow of a golden age.

If asked to name the moment when the Nicklaus era came to an end, a good many golfers would surely think back to the 1982 U.S. Open at Pebble Beach, where Nicklaus seemed to be on the verge of winning his twentieth major championship, a number that would nicely round off his monumental career. Nicklaus had played stalwart golf from tee to green, but at the age of forty-two, he wasn't dropping as many putts as he used to. During the first three rounds of play, Nicklaus had made only six birdies; and then on Sunday, he suddenly found his putting stroke, made six more birdies, and pulled away from everyone but his old nemesis, Tom Watson, who was still on the course. They were tied at four under par. As Nicklaus entered the scorer's tent to check his card, he saw on the television monitor that Watson hooked his tee shot at the 17th into the tangled rough around the green. The ball was on a downslope, sitting as deep in the grass as an egg in a nest. Even if he popped the ball out cleanly, Watson had only a few feet of very slippery green in which to stop it. From that lie, Nicklaus thought, Watson didn't have a prayer of getting the ball in the hole. With luck Watson might save his par, but a bogey was more likely—and a bogey meant that he'd have to birdie the difficult 18th to salvage a tie.

Nicklaus made these gratifying calculations and began to verify his scorecard. Then came the jubilant roar from the vicinity of the 17th, and he glanced back up at the monitor to see Watson dancing at the edge of the green like a man on hot coals. The ball was in the cup, and the Open was Watson's. Nicklaus was waiting to congratulate him when he holed his final putt, and the image of those two—the Golden Bear, now the Olden Bear, accepting his defeat with good grace, his arm flung around the shoulders of a grinning, gap-toothed, exultant Watson—captures the essence of one of the most stirring rivalries in the history of the game.

Pebble Beach wasn't the first time that Watson had

snatched a major championship away from Nicklaus. The two first squared off at the 1977 Masters, and later that summer they tangled again in the British Open at Turnberry, a battle that passed immediately into the realm of legend. They both played inspired golf. Tied after two rounds of play, they were paired together on the third day and matched each other stroke for sensational stroke, shooting identical 65s. On the last day, Watson, after trailing for most of the round, brought in another 65 and won by a single stroke. Both of them had shattered to smithereens the old record total for the British Open, and left the rest of the field so far behind that Hubert Green, who finished third, 11 strokes back, was moved to remark, "I won the golf tournament. I don't know what game those other two guys were playing."

But of course Green did know, as did everyone else, that they were playing for the crown, and for the next five years, Watson was the one who wore it. During that period he won more tournaments and more money than any other golfer; but in the four major championships, Nicklaus was still dangerous. Between Turnberry and Pebble Beach, even though Nicklaus kept trimming back his tournament schedule, he and Watson won the same number of majors—three. It was no secret that Nicklaus regarded the majors as the building blocks of his career, and even when he seemed to be playing lackluster golf, he was still able to bring his game to a peak for the big events. Between them Nicklaus and Watson dominated the majors for a period of five years; they staged another of their donnybrooks at the 1981 Masters, which Watson won by playing tenacious golf on the last day. In those two golf seemed to have the equivalent of Queen Victoria and Prince Edward, the crown prince ready to mount the throne and the formidable old monarch unwilling to step aside.

Watson's victory at Pebble Beach, however, had an air of finality about it. It was the fourth time Nicklaus had come up short, and his years were beginning to show. His putting was the telltale sign. The two great champions before him, Hogan and Palmer, had faded in exactly the same way, losing their touch on the greens long before their other talents deserted them. When Nicklaus won the Memorial tournament in 1984—a tournament that he frankly created in the image and likeness of the Masters, played on a course that he himself designed, in his hometown of Columbus, Ohio—he seemed to have engineered the appropriate sentimental finale. His eldest son, Jackie, caddied for him at the Memorial, a hint that he might be ready to settle into a role as a sort of benevolent father figure or elder statesman. There were rumors, as there had been for years, of his imminent retirement; and a few writers were beginning to call upon Nicklaus to bow out gracefully, before the inevitable decline set in and tarnished the memories of his great and now bygone deeds. Nicklaus, however, kept showing up for the majors and a few other tournaments, attracting loyal galleries whenever he played. With the possible exception of a few die-hard fans, no one really expected him to win again—a few die-hard fans and, as it turned out, Nicklaus himself.

Watson's win at Pebble Beach, his first U.S. Open victory, was supposed to have been a breakthrough, and the oracles of the game were prophesying a majestic future for him. He was only thirty-two years old, and well on his way to amassing the credentials of an authentically great golfer. On the championship ledger, he had already caught up with Lee Trevino, and he wasn't far behind Sam Snead (who won seven majors), Arnold Palmer (eight), Gary Player (nine), and Ben Hogan (nine). Within a month he had won another British Open, much to his surprise; he was in the clubhouse at Royal Troon when two younger players came unstuck and made him a gift of the championship. A special star always seemed to watch over Watson at the British Open, and when he won again at Royal Birkdale—it was the only tournament he won in 1983—he found himself in a position to tie one of the most sacrosanct records in golf. Back in the days of the hickory shaft, Harry Vardon had won a record six British Opens; but Vardon was the only man to have done so, and nobody else, not even Nicklaus, had carried off one of the major championships more than five times (both Nicklaus and Walter Hagen had won five

PGAs, and Peter Thomson had five victories in the British Open).

The 1984 British Open was played at St. Andrews. If Watson needed any more incentive, he certainly had it. Not only is St. Andrews where the recorded history of the game began, but the players with whom Watson could now rightly expect to be compared—Vardon, Jones, and Nicklaus—had all prevailed there. Moreover, having already won on the other four Scottish courses over which the British Open is played, Watson could complete another sort of slam, a Scottish slam, at St. Andrews.

From the start of the tournament he was in the thick of things, and halfway through the final round of play the Open turned into a duel between him and Ballesteros. It was touch and go for several holes, and Watson came to what is perhaps the most famous hole in golf, the 17th at St. Andrews, the Road Hole, knowing that he needed a par to keep pace with Ballesteros. He didn't get it. He pushed his approach shot far to the right, and it finished in a little rut in the surface of the road only 2 feet from a stone wall. With no room for a backswing, Watson could only jab at it, and the ball rolled some 30 feet past the pin. Watson took two putts to get down. Since Ballesteros had birdied the 18th, Watson needed an eagle 2 on that same hole in order to tie. After a big drive, he paced off the yardage all the way to the flag, an unusually deliberate gesture, and one that showed just how badly he wanted the miracle that would bring him that sixth title. It was not to be, and Watson had not won a tournament since.

Which brings us back to Ballesteros. The Spaniard didn't win any major titles in 1985, and with his suspension, the death of his father, and his lack of competitive play, he might have been expected to show some signs of distraction or uncertainty when he arrived at Augusta. He didn't. He was ready to play. It was as if he had said to himself, "All right, Beman suspended me, so I'll show him. I'll come over and win the Masters." Another victory here would make it difficult for anyone to deny him the unofficial title he coveted, *el major golfista del mundo.* During one of his press conferences before the tournament, Ballesteros seemed to repeat his Lake City prediction, saying, "I come to Augusta to win."

He was the man to beat in the 1986 Masters.

# 2

## On the Terrace

The city of Augusta literally puts itself out for the Masters. Nearly all of the golfers and the thousands of out-of-town fans stay in private houses that have been vacated for the week by their owners. The motels for miles around are booked solid, and the restaurants and watering holes are braced for the most profitable week of the year. Every local you meet hopes that the weather will cooperate and the azaleas will bloom, and the whole place—no longer the sleepy Southern town it may have been once upon a time, but a perky little Sunbelt city with its fair share of mini malls, prosperous subdivisions, fast-food franchises, and foreign restaurants—gets into the spirit of the tournament (or, as they still say in Georgia, the "toonamint"). They are proud of the Masters in Augusta, and yes, they do hustle Masters dollars with some enthusiasm; but for a big-time sports event, the Masters still has a cozy, down-home feeling, the feeling of a vast college reunion. You may not know everyone there, but you know why they're there and what you all have in common.

Television coverage of the Masters begins with the slow, stately progress of a camera down Magnolia Lane. A good many visitors, too, begin their tournament with a ritual stroll down this fabled passage. It is the main entrance to the Augusta National Golf Club, but during Masters week only a few official cars are permitted to use it. The ordinary badge-holder parks in one of the lots off Washington Road and enters by a less picturesque route that leads past the equipment sheds, the communications vans, and all the other support facilities.

The visitor who wants the full, heady effect of the place, however, makes his way to Magnolia Lane. The magnolias aren't in bloom in April, but their branches interlace overhead and form a leafy tunnel. To either side there is a practice range, though only one of them, the West Range, is used by the competitors in the tournament; the East Range is too short. Beyond the trees, then, you hear that satisfying *thwack* of golf balls being hit and hit hard, and up ahead you see the sunlit white clubhouse with its cupola and veranda. It stands behind an oval lawn where, on a small grassy mound, a bed of bright yellow flowers is in bloom. The bed is cut in the outline of the United States, and a yellow flagstick is planted in its lower right, or southeast, corner, to mark the location of Augusta. The map and flagstick, of course, are the logo of the club.

The clubhouse is smaller than you might imagine, and less imposing. It still looks like what it once was, the residence of a well-off family, not the mansion of a grandee. Back when it was built in 1854, it was called, simply enough, the Manor, and before Bobby Jones bought the property, the house belonged to the Berckman family, who ran a large nursery on the land that is now the golf course. Because you approach it from the relative dimness of the magnolias, everything about the clubhouse—the two chimneys, the striped awning, the green shutters, the railings on the veranda—seems in curiously sharp focus. The place is actually plain, or at least understated: its charm doesn't depend on any adornments but is built into its clean, pure, symmetrical lines.

The pink azaleas are blazing away to either side of the entrance, and a long, low addition sprawls off in either direction. With the right sort of badge, you can continue your progress straight on through the clubhouse, which is as functional and unfussy inside as it is outside. You emerge on the grassy terrace in the back, where the tables and umbrellas have been set up, and where the big live oaks are unfurling their fuzzy new golden leaves. This is the same path Bobby Jones followed when he first visited the place, and the valley that sweeps away below you is the same view he was so smitten by. "It seemed that this land had been lying here for years waiting for some- one to lay a golf course upon it," he wrote afterward, and now that golf course exists. Two greens, the 9th and 18th, are right in front of you, and two others lie at the bottom of the natural amphitheater, which is surely one of the most beautiful sport- ing arenas in the world. The fairways are a lustrous green— actually two shades of green: a dark green where they have been mowed with the grain, a lighter green where the mower went against the grain. That distinctive striping is repeated, in miniature, on the greens and tees, which are smooth enough to putt on. What takes your breath away as you drink in the view is how immaculate it all is, and, most of all, the monumen- tal scale. The place is vast. The breadth of the fairways, the height of the pines, the tumbling expanse of the greens, the huge, gleaming bunkers—if giants walked the earth, and played golf, this is where they would play.

Once you have inhaled deeply of this rarefied air, you are ready to see some golf. Most visitors seem to follow the line of least resistance and head down the hill toward Rae's Creek and Amen Corner, those three holes, the 11th, 12th, and 13th, where the Masters has so often been won or lost. The water comes into play on each hole. Twice, in 1940 and again in 1951, Sam Snead looked like winning the tournament when he came to the 11th, put a ball in the water, and staggered away with a quadruple bogey 8. The 12th, according to Jack Nicklaus, is the most demanding tournament hole in the world; listed on the card at 155 yards, it plays straight over the creek to a long, narrow green that runs away from the golfer at the angle of a clock's hands at ten past two. Nicklaus doesn't like to gamble on this hole, but in 1981, holding a two-shot lead over Watson in the Saturday round, he dumped one into the water, took a double bogey, and eventually lost the tournament by two strokes. As for the 13th, it was the scene of Curtis Strange's disaster in 1985. A par 5 that is only 465 yards long, it requires a second shot over the creek that winds around the front of the green—but Strange didn't make it as far as the green. He waded into the water and hacked the ball out for a bogey, and two holes down the line, at the 15th—the other short par 5 on the back nine that invites the golfer to attempt a carry over water—he dropped another ball into the drink, made another bogey, and gave away the tournament.

Every Masters buff will have his own memories, not all of them having to do with the winning or losing of the championship. During the practice days before the start of the 1986 Masters, for instance, the visitor to Amen Corner could follow a piece of living history—the old champ himself, Arnold Palmer, playing one of his tune-up rounds. When he appeared in the fairway to play his approach to the 11th, he was recognizable by that familiar swing; his snatching follow-through still looked like the effort of a man to set a hook in a trophy fish. A small, appreciative crowd applauded when he dropped his tee shot at the 12th on the green, and he cracked out a fair drive at the 13th (you can follow a player all the way around Amen Corner by moving only a hundred yards or so through a stand of pines). He still had a poke of 220 yards to carry Rae's Creek. He was playing with a young pro who'd recently won his first tournament, and someone in the crowd asked, "Who's that with Arnie?" His companion replied, "I don't know. The epitome of anonymity."

Close up, with his hair lying on his forehead in short gray bangs, Palmer bore a resemblance to Caesar. He hitched his pants and pulled out his 3-wood. He was going for it. Hitting the ball flush, he started it out to the right and drew it into the flag. "Go, go, go," everyone was saying as the ball started down against a backdrop of azaleas and towering pines. It landed on the bank just short of the green and kicked back into the water. Shrugging, Palmer dropped another ball, hitched his pants again, and smashed out a carbon copy of that first shot—same low trajectory, same draw, same line, but this time he had added the five extra yards. The ball landed on the green and ran up close to the pin, and Palmer grinned for all he was worth. The applause was more than polite. It was just the kind of exhilarating golf shot everyone comes to Augusta to see.

By Tuesday, all eighty-eight competitors had arrived in Augusta to get in their practice rounds. They all went about their preparations seriously, though not all were as serious as Langer, the defending champion. He'd come equipped with a rolling measuring device, a wheel on a stick, and he was getting exact distances from the various pin locations to the edges of the greens. "This is a course where you have to know every square inch," he said, and apparently he wasn't kidding. Most of the golfers were content simply to pace off distances around the green and enter them in their yardage books (the Masters yardage book isn't one of your slick four-color brochures; it has a nice homemade quality, with pen-and-ink drawings, and the water hazards are indicated by tiny wavelets, cheerful-looking fish, and the warning $H_2O$). They spent far less time on their full shots—the practice range was the place to work on the swing—than they did checking out the greens and the areas just off the greens. There has always been a lot of wisdom at Augusta about places where you do *not* want to miss a green.

In fact, the whole course takes some knowing, though at first glance it seems straightforward enough. It has the same architectural virtues as the clubhouse—the same clean, uncluttered lines, the same classical simplicity of design. Bobby Jones was an "extravagant admirer" of St. Andrews, but it is difficult at first to see what Augusta National has in common with St. Andrews, a course that also resembles its clubhouse, the Royal and Ancient clubhouse, in its defiant intricacy and weathered angularity. The more you study Augusta National, though, and the more you watch it baffle the best golfers in the world, the more you come to appreciate its subtleties. The main hazards are perfectly obvious, but the small ones, the ones that can eat up the strokes, are almost invisible until a golfer has experienced them.

Take, for instance, the 13th hole. The moment a golfer steps onto the tee, he knows that two good shots will put him on the green with a good chance for a birdie and a crack at an eagle. The hole is a dogleg left, and the first decision he faces is how close to cut the corner. If he can draw it daringly around the trees, he not only shortens the hole but places his ball in the only level area of the fairway. The right-hand side of the fairway is banked like the turn of a speedway, and the farther right he goes, the more steeply it is banked. (First-time visitors to the Masters are invariably surprised by how much up and down there is on the course.) Right off the tee, then, the player is tempted to flirt with the trees and the creek that runs along the left side of the fairway. The player who plays a safer shot out to the right might be able to get home in two, but he will most likely find himself in Palmer's shoes, needing to play an all-out, first-class shot. Furthermore, he will play it from a hanging lie or a hook lie; and it is much harder to make a hooking ball settle down softly on a green. There is some room to err to the left—but there are bunkers to the left, and a slippery grassy bank leading up to an undulating green. The golfer who puts a ball at the foot of it might as well forget his birdie, and by now the hole has him wondering whether he might be better off to lay up.

The 13th, in short, teases a golfer all the way from tee to green. It offers him alternate routes to the flag, one risky and one safe. That is the essence of strategic design, of course; the architect leaves the strategy up to the player. On a course of penal design, the architect has charted one route, and one route only, and the player has no choice but to follow it. He who errs on a penal course is punished swiftly and harshly; a strategic course punishes a bad shot in proportion to the error. To put it another way, a strategic course is seductive; a penal course is sadistic.

Bobby Jones and his collaborator, Alister Mackenzie, were of one mind about the Augusta National golf course. They wanted a course that could be played, with pleasure, by members of the club, and that would at the same time provide top-caliber players with a thorough examination. A strategic course it would have to be. Mackenzie routed the holes, and Jones hit out thousands of balls to test the shot values of each one. They agreed to leave out many of the hazards that have theatrical value but don't always add much to the intrinsic difficulty or interest of a hole. There are, for instance, only 45 bunkers on the course—as opposed, say, to over 200 at Oakmont, one of the traditional sites of the U.S. Open. The rough is hardly more intimidating than an ordinary, well-kept suburban lawn. There are five water hazards, all of them on the back nine, but you don't have to risk a long carry except at the two par 3s, the 12th and the 16th—and neither of them is particularly long, not from the members' tees.

But if a golfer does find the rough too often or keeps playing to the wrong side of the fairway, if he doesn't *think* his way through the course, he won't stay in contention very long. He won't be able to get his ball into the right spot on the glassy greens—the right spot is always below the hole—and he won't make his birdies. The key to a good showing in the Masters is position on the large, rolling greens, and the influence of the greens radiates backward, so to speak, since the best way to plan an attack is from the hole back to the tee. Taking the pin placement into account, the golfer tries to figure out first of all where an ideal approach would finish (and also, since all golfers are mortal, what kind of trouble he might be in with a less-than-ideal approach). The next step, still working backward, is to consider the best angle for the approach shot and the proper landing area for a drive. There's little percentage, for instance, in banging a big drive down the left side of the first fairway—not unless a player fancies coming at the flag straight over the only bunker around the green. At the par-5 second hole, the man who wants to give himself a birdie or eagle opportunity has to be on the opposite side of the fairway from the flag, so that he can attempt to thread his long approach between the two bunkers. He can't hold the green if he flies the bunkers, and if he's on the wrong side—well, it's easy as pie to three-putt from 50 or 60 feet away.

And so it goes from one hole to the next. Augusta National is a golf course that puts a premium on judgment. Not too many years ago, when Palmer and Nicklaus seemed to take turns winning the Masters, it had a reputation as a paradise for the long hitter who could also draw the ball (all but two of the doglegs are to the left). You could step up and whale away, or so the theory went. It is true that the power hitter has a greater advantage in the Masters than on the tighter courses used in the U.S. Open or the PGA; but every year there are more players who get home at the par 5s and reach the long par 4s with relatively short irons. Increasingly, Augusta National has come to be seen as a "second shot" golf course, one that places unremitting demands on iron play and putting.

Every member of the press corps is given a copy of a small green booklet called *The Records of the Masters Tournament*, and it does contain a few records. Each year's tournament is written up in a few paragraphs, and there are several pages filled with scores; but the last pages of the book are devoted to bread-and-butter letters written by Masters winners. Some are addressed to Hord Hardin, the present chairman of the Masters, and some are addressed to Bob Jones. Most of them, however, are directed to Cliff Roberts.

From the beginning, Roberts was the man behind the scenes—and not always that far behind them. He was the chairman of the tournament from its inception until his death in 1977 when, sick and perhaps mindful of Jones's terribly drawn-out illness, he shot himself on the club's grounds. By all accounts, Roberts ran the tournament the way the pope runs the Church, with the presumption of infallibility. No one—neither Jones nor his other great friend and club member, President Eisenhower—could tell Cliff Roberts what to do. On the contrary, he told them. One of the stories that lives on is how, at a club meeting, Ike had the temerity to speak up about the tree that grows in the middle of the 17th fairway. "You're out of order," said Roberts, and adjourned the meeting.

Roberts is remembered, too, for having interrupted a television announcer who made the mistake of referring to the Augusta National Country Club. "This is no damn country club," Roberts growled into the microphones. He fired another broadcaster for referring to a Masters crowd as a "mob." He saw to it that no telecast mentioned money on the air, as in "This putt is for fifty thousand dollars." The emphasis in the

Masters telecasts was to be on tradition, and Roberts went to New York every year to screen the full tapes with the CBS brass. At his request he was served tea and Oreo cookies with the white stuff scraped off. Everybody worshiped Bobby Jones, but they were afraid of Cliff Roberts, and kowtowed to him. Near the end of his life, when he had to fill out a form to be reinstated as an amateur, Jones listed his own profession as "assistant." As his employer, he put down Cliff Roberts.

The fanatical Roberts, not surprisingly, rubbed a good many people the wrong way, but nobody dared to criticize the Masters. Indeed, the way Roberts ran it, there was almost nothing to criticize. Under his guidance the Masters won the reputation it has kept as the best-run of all golf tournaments. Perhaps the most significant Roberts innovation was the use of scoreboards, posted so that players and spectators alike could keep abreast of the play. The Masters also pioneered the use of red numbers and green numbers to show where a player stood in relation to par, red indicating a figure below par, green the number of shots he was over par. Since the course was the site of a major tournament every year, Roberts made sure that the spectators—they were to be called patrons— were well served. Unobtrusive and natural-looking mounds were built at key locations, especially around the greens, to make sure that the galleries had an unobstructed view. For the same reason periscopes were outlawed. Permanent comfort stations were built, and hidden away in stands of trees. The concession stands were likewise discreetly placed, and painted green, of course. Everything that wasn't alive was painted green. Every cent of money that was taken in went back into improving the course and the tournament. It is even said of Roberts that one year when the azaleas began to bloom too early, he sent out members of the grounds crew to pack their roots with ice.

Whenever I hear Cliff Roberts stories, I think of Ludwig, the petty Bavarian king. He was quite mad, but he built the castle, Neuschwanstein, which still stands as the fantastic epitome of what a castle ought to be—just as the Masters somehow epitomizes what golf ought to be.

* * *

Like everything else at the Augusta National Golf Club, the practice range is handsomely groomed and appointed. Bordered on one side by Magnolia Lane and on the other by a high hedge, it has room enough for about twenty players to practice comfortably. The teeing area is divided into two levels by a low stone retaining wall, and it is marked off by the same small sticks of cordwood that are used as tee markers on the course. The first thing a caddy does when he enters the range—the player is usually a few steps behind, signing autographs—is to station his bag at one of the vacant slots, and then he reports to the white shed at the back of the range, under a live oak tree, to pick up a few bags of balls. They are all brand-new, freshly washed, and sorted according to make.

When the golfer makes his appearance, all he has to do is put on his glove and he's ready to go to work. There are three greens for him to aim at, each with a flagstick, one 100 yards out, the second 150 yards out, and the third just over 200 yards away. About 50 yards beyond the last green, there is a 12-foot net to keep balls from flying into Washington Road. A few balls clear that net, but they are caught in a second, higher net about 10 yards still farther back.

No matter how many times you have seen professional golfers honing their skills, you still cannot believe how hard, how high, and how straight they hit the ball. The people who do not play golf, the ones who like to argue that golf is not a real sport and golfers aren't true athletes, ought to sit in the bleachers behind the practice range or better yet, stand directly behind the golfers, as the caddies do, and just watch for a while. When a pro swings it, a golf club becomes one of the fastest-moving things in sport. It may look as if the golfer has taken an effortless swing, but look again—look at the long gouge of the divot, and watch how the ball explodes off the clubface. It's just a white streak until it approaches the highest point of its trajectory and begins to slow down. Even the sound of a pro's swing is intimidating, not a silken rending of the air but a metallic rip. And when the clubface meets the ball, it makes a noise like a ripe tomato hitting a fence.

After you've watched shot after shot rain down on the flagsticks, you may begin to wonder why so many of the players seem to be working so hard. To the ordinary golfer their results look astounding, but they shake their heads, and mutter, and spend a few moments making some minute adjustment in their hip turn, or setup, or take-away. Then they drag up another ball, hit it with what appears to be exactly the same line and trajectory, and make more invisible adjustments. As you watch them—and the same is true when you hear them discuss their golf swings—you can't help thinking that they are all as sensitive as the princess who felt the pea through a hundred mattresses. She couldn't sleep until it was removed, and they don't rest from their toils until their swings are absolutely perfect.

At this point you may also begin to wonder how golfers who are so powerful and accurate could ever miss a fairway or green, or shoot a score higher than par. The answer, of course, is that there is all the difference in the world between playing a competitive round and hitting balls on a range. It is the difference, to borrow a phrase from Mark Twain, between the lightning and the lightning bug. One of the best ways to appreciate the pressure of tournament golf is to spend an hour watching these players when the pressure is off. They all look like champs.

Still, it was easy enough to distinguish among the swings on display at Augusta. Tom Kite, for instance, was usually down at the far right of the range, grinding away. Known as one of the most disciplined players in a sport that prizes the work ethic, Kite was fine-tuning a swing that was already a model of efficiency; and in the language of the pros, *efficient* is a term of the highest praise. There wasn't a single wasted motion in his swing or, for that matter, in his entire routine. By the time he'd run through his irons, setting up each ball beside the last divot, he'd removed a square of turf about two feet by two feet. You couldn't have done a more meticulous job with a ruler and a chisel.

Yet if you compared Tom Kite's swing to, say, Tom Watson's, it looked almost too applied. Kite came to a dead stop when he addressed the ball; Watson moved into his take-away with a series of small, eager steps, like a high-strung thoroughbred moving into the starting gate—he may have the best footwork among the pros. Altogether, his swing was more free and uninhibited than Kite's, though between shots he kept moving the club rather stiffly away from the ball, trying to make sure that he fanned the clubhead open to the proper degree. A closed clubface leads to a hook, of course, and a hook had been his besetting flaw. One more thing about Watson: Even though he was trying to encode his body with a whole set of small commands, he managed to hit out three balls for every two that the other players hit. Everything about Watson's game—his walk, the tempo of his backswing, the time he spends on a putt—has always been speedy, but still, he looked impatient on the range.

Greg Norman, a.k.a. the Great White Shark, the Australian with the shoulders of a stevedore and the waist of a dancer, was belting out the prodigious drives for which he was famous. He was also famous for his platinum hair, his cheerful irreverence, and his attacking style of play. Every time he sent a ball soaring into the distant nets—and he was reaching the back net—a small, awestruck voice inside your head exclaimed, "But that is huge! That is huge!" Norman himself seemed to savor his power as much as the fans, who kept urging him to drive one into Washington Road. One of the reasons for his enormous popularity, surely, was the unabashed gusto he brought to the game.

At the finish of his swing, Norman carried his hands high overhead and his back was arched in a curve like a longbow. His right foot had slid close to his left, where it ended up *en pointe*, like a ballerina's, an oddly dainty conclusion to such an exuberant blast. With his looks and his power, Norman was the kind of golfer who inspired Bunyanesque stories, and one of them making the rounds was that his wife, Laura, after watching him pound out drive after drive, said, "Greg, you use clubs other than your driver. Why don't you practice with them?"

He'd begun his practice routine by running through his irons, and he finished it off by chipping a few balls—chipping them, mischievously, into the small stone stairway in the retaining wall, where they boinged about like stray atoms.

Ballesteros was a good deal more sober. His brother, Vicente, who had accompanied him from Spain to caddy for him, invariably appeared on the tee several minutes before Seve arrived, and staked out a position to the far left of the range. Aficionados of the bullfight say that every bull seeks a spot in the ring where he is most comfortable; the Spanish word for this preferential sense of place is *querencia,* and Ballesteros evidently shared it. He strode onto the tee, hopped down from the upper level, and proceeded to play out a sequence of shots according to an inscrutable private agenda. He chose his own targets, aiming at the flagstick only when it suited him, playing most shots cater-cornered, never hitting more than three in a row with the same shape. Some were high, some low, some were faded and some drawn; but he did *something* with virtually every shot. "Golf is not supposed to be mechanical," he said when asked about his routine. "A golfer is not a machine."

All these shots were produced by variations of the same lyrical swing. It was something to behold. The pedigree of that swing could be traced back through Sam Snead, the purveyor of aesthetic delight in his generation, to Bobby Jones, who enraptured onlookers with the sweetness of his stroke. So did Ballesteros. He simply flowed through the ball, and he made the golf swing look not merely effortless but elegant. The elements of his swing—his tempo, rhythm, and balance—were so nicely fused that it was difficult to see how he managed to generate so much clubhead speed; you almost expected his shots to drop just at the front of the teeing area. They didn't. He was hitting what looked like a 4-iron out as far as the most distant green, and his fairway woods—they were metal woods—were jumping into the netting on the first hop. Ballesteros has always claimed that power comes from the right side, but his swing also has a long arc produced by an exceptionally full shoulder turn; in his follow-through, his right shoulder was actually pointed toward his target.

There is almost no disagreement that Ballesteros has the most beautiful swing in the game, and several players interrupted their own labors to watch him for a few moments. Some of them were no doubt admiring what they saw, but they also wanted to see whether he was rusty after his layoff. One professional who played a round with him answered that question: "I don't think Seve's ever rusty."

For Jack Nicklaus, the short walk from the locker room to the practice range was an exercise in both penmanship and discretion. Autograph-seekers homed in on him, and he tried to oblige as many of them as he could, dashing off his signature—a beefy *J*, a sinuous *N*—on the Masters programs and cap visors thrust in front of him. Over the years Nicklaus has learned to accommodate these requests graciously, and he always seemed to have his eye peeled for the shy youngster hanging back at the edge of the crowd. "Let me see that program, son," he'd say, and as he signed it, he'd ask the wonderstruck boy a question or two about his own golf game. Nicklaus, of course, has had years to grow accustomed to his celebrity, but his easy, natural manner with his admirers, especially the young ones, went far beyond the call of duty. He genuinely seemed to be enjoying himself as he shuffled along at the center of what looked like a slow-moving rugby scrum.

Nicklaus's son Jackie had come to Augusta to caddy for him, and he was rarely more than a few steps away, carrying the familiar green MacGregor bag. At twenty-four, Jackie was much closer in age to most of the competitors than his father was; and even in his white caddy coveralls, he *looked* more like them, tall and supple, while Nicklaus Senior was distinctly portly. Almost twenty years ago, he had gone on a diet to get rid of the Fat Jack label, but now he was eating ice cream and steak, and his weight was up from 170 to 190. Since his willpower had been almost as renowned as his playing ability, one had to wonder if he'd decided, at the age of forty-six, to let things slide a little.

After his dismal performance on the winter circuit, there had been renewed speculation about when he might retire,

and the Masters brought it to a crescendo. In the seven tournaments he'd entered in 1986, he'd missed the cut in three and
withdrawn from a fourth when his mother-in-law died. His
best finish had been a tie for 39th at the Hawaiian Open.
Because he had been such a potent force at the Masters for so
many years, nearly every sportswriter with a pretournament
story to file felt called upon to point out how poorly he'd been
playing, and some, like Tom McCollister of the Atlanta *Journal,* went even further; they said he was through. One of
Nicklaus's good friends, John Montgomery, clipped McCollister's article and taped it to the refrigerator in the house
Nicklaus had rented for the week.

The other news items about Nicklaus had mostly to do
with his business woes. Back in the fall, he'd come to a parting
of the ways with Chuck Perry, the longtime chief executive
officer of his company, Golden Bear International. Nicklaus,
with his usual candor, said that his company was "a mess," and
admitted that his tangled affairs had been a distraction. Rumors were flying about the amount of money he stood to lose
in a couple of troubled golf course and real estate deals, and
when it was learned that he was about to sign a five-year
contract with ABC-TV to do special golf programs, there were
whispers that Nicklaus, often referred to as the richest athlete
in history, was in a financial crunch. No matter how much or
how little truth these speculations held, the fact was that Nicklaus's once-seamless reputation as the man who succeeded in
everything was beginning to unravel around the edges.

The low point for Nicklaus came in early March when he
tied for 47th at the Doral Open, a tournament he had won
twice, and where he counted on playing well. He was hitting
the ball "all over the world," and when he missed a green, his
short game was too slipshod to enable him to recover. Royally
exasperated, he took his troubles to Jack Grout, who had
taught him to play golf when he was ten, and had been his only
coach throughout his career. One of the fundamentals that
Grout had drummed into his star pupil was that the only func-
tion of the hands during a golf swing was to hold on to the club;
but Nicklaus had gotten too handsy. "I had to get my hands out

of the swing," Nicklaus said. "I'd been too violent with my hands going through the hitting area." One result of this exaggerated hand action was that he'd lost all feel for the clubhead, and with it the touch that a tournament player must have to give himself birdie opportunities; five yards too much, or too little, takes the ball out of birdie range.

Grout suggested other adjustments—a more deliberate change of direction at the top of the backswing, for one, and a taller stance at address. It's difficult enough for a golfer to incorporate one change into his swing without ruining it, but Nicklaus was working on half a dozen things at once, and he wasn't just trying to patch up his full swing, either. He was also trying to bring his chipping up to speed, and his short-game coach was son Jackie, who'd recently spent a week in Puerto Rico working on his chipping and pitching with Chi Chi Rodriguez. A fine golfer in his own right, Jackie had played for his college team at the University of North Carolina and won the North and South Amateur Championship, but he knew that if he wanted to compete successfully as a professional, he was going to have to improve his short game. During their practice sessions together, Nicklaus began to admire the Rodriguez method, and tried it himself. Essentially, it involved keeping the hands ahead of the clubface throughout the swing to promote a firm striking of the ball. The one weakness in the Nicklaus arsenal had always been the little finesse shots, and when he saw Jackie hitting them with such confidence, he wasn't too stubborn to learn something from him.

On top of everything else, Nicklaus was using a new offset putter with a cast aluminum head about three times the size of a normal putter. It was manufactured by his own company, MacGregor, and Nicklaus, sounding like a physicist, had been convinced to try it because it had "the largest possible moment of inertia and the smallest dispersion factor." Tom Watson took one look at it and said, "Looks like you're going out to kill something for dinner, Jack."

In the month just before the Masters, then, Nicklaus had tried not only to forget his business worries but to overhaul his long game, his short game, and his putting—to catch not a second wind but something more like a tenth or twelfth wind. Many an aging athlete has tried to stave off the inevitable, but Nicklaus was actually beginning to see some results. On the practice tee, he seemed to be in a relaxed, garrulous mood, talking over each shot with Jackie but still, as he set up for each, invoking the familiar Nicklausian concentration. In the nearly thirty years that he had been hitting golf balls in full view of the public, no one had ever seen him give anything less than an all-out effort, and he wasn't starting now.

His swing began, as always, with the solid placement of his feet and the series of waggles, each one descending closer to the ball, and each one a little shorter than the one before; by the time he rested the club on the grass, he seemed to have brought himself under the same tremendous compression as the ball lying there at his feet. When you think of most golfers' swings, you think of the follow-through; but it is Nicklaus's address that impresses itself most on the memory. His take-away started with that slight turn of the head to the rear, and then, in midflight, you could see two other Nicklaus trade-marks; the left heel lifted high off the ground and the semifly-ing elbow. At the top of his backswing, he looked spring-weighted, and he was really unloading on the ball. As he would say after the tournament, he could feel himself gathering up his force at the top of his backswing, and he was getting a kick out of unleashing it. Publicly, he said only that he would like, occasionally, to play as well as he used to. Privately, his hopes were rising, and one night before the tournament he told his wife, Barbara, "I think I found that fellow out there that I used to know."

On Wednesday afternoon, the practice days came to their traditional close with the Par-3 Contest. The golfers obviously welcomed the event as an eve-of-the-battle diversion, and larked around the sumptuous little course to the east of the clubhouse. The air was crystalline and cool, but the azaleas were beginning to bloom along the banks of DeSoto Springs Pond, the centerpiece of the course.

With a star-studded field, the Par-3 Contest was a showcase affair, as much a pageant as a competition. Payne Stewart upstaged everybody, sartorially speaking, when he appeared in formal attire—black tie, wing collar, starched shirt with studs, and of course, black knickers. The seventy-four-year-old Byron Nelson cruised through, showing plenty of spring in his step, accompanied by his protégé, Tom Watson, and by Scott Verplanck, the amateur who gave golf fans such a jolt when he won the 1985 Western Open. Gary Player got the loudest cheer of the afternoon when he made a hole-in-one at the seventh, but the little physical-fitness advocate didn't leap or dance; he expressed his joy isometrically. Hal Sutton left a shot five inches from the hole, and Ray Floyd parked one only a foot away from the pin. Lee Trevino, Hale Irwin, and Tommy Nakajima also won nearest-to-the-flagstick honors. Greg Norman was whooping it up for his playing partner, Gary Koch, who had a hot hand; and Bernhard Langer, known as a stone face, got into the spirit of things with a Teutonic version of body English. There were so many notable golfers, so many on-target shots, and so much general good humor that the sound of applause kept rippling through the crowd all afternoon. For anyone who wanted to see the world's best golfers disporting themselves, to see them at close hand and before the strain of the tournament began to tell, the Par-3 Contest was the place to be.

Gary Koch won the contest, though he had to play three extra holes to beat Augusta's native son, Larry Mize. The two were tied at 23 after the regulation nine holes, and in the playoff they showed signs of superstition—no winner of the Par-3 Contest had ever gone on to win the main event, and you could hardly blame Koch and Mize for playing raggedly. When Koch knocked in a long putt on the third playoff hole, he had to feel a little bit like the kid in the card game who ends up holding the old maid.

One of the few players who played hooky from the contest was Ballesteros, who wanted to get in one last practice round. He was nevertheless in a playful mood, and why not? This Wednesday was his twenty-ninth birthday, and his virtuoso skills had never looked more impressive. On the 13th hole, he drove to the right, underneath the trees, and the fans there urged him to go for the green. With low-hanging branches in front of him, he didn't have much of a shot, but he invented one, a 3-wood that started out like a clothesline, stayed under the branches, then kicked into a different gear when it was out in the open, gaining altitude and finally touching down softly on the distant green. At the 16th, he gave the onlookers another treat, skipping 2-iron shots across the water until one of them bounded onto the green and snuggled close to the flagstick. When he came off the course and sat down for a short press interview, he wanted to joke about the $50 Nassau he'd won from Ben Crenshaw and Gary Player earlier in the week: "It's the most money I made all year."

Before he gave up the microphone, though, he had chided Masters officials for not inviting more European players to the tournament, and reminded everyone that the Europeans had won the Ryder Cup. He ticked off a list of several players he thought deserved to be in the field, and he couldn't resist taking another swat at Deane Beman (who, incidentally, was the most conspicuous absentee at this Masters). After repeating his barb that Beman was "a little man trying to be a big man," he said, "Let's forget Deane Beman. The Masters is more important than Deane Beman."

He hadn't come to Augusta to worry about his suspension. Why had he come? "I come to this place to enjoy the hospitality and to win the Masters. I feel strong mentally and physically. I am ready to win."

# 3

# Thursday

On Thursday morning there was one final ceremony to observe. While the contestants were getting in their last licks on the practice range, a compact gentleman in cream knickers stepped onto the first tee, beaming at the applause that greeted him. He was Gene Sarazen, of course, and his playing partner in the crimson sweater and Panama hat was Sam Snead. This year's honorary starters, they looked perky and robust as they prepared to play the opening shots of the tournament, blowing on their hands to warm them. They would be driving into a brisk southwest wind, and Sarazen, without so much as a practice swing, stepped up and spanked his first shot off to the left. He was awarded a Mulligan, perhaps the first in Masters history, and this time he socked the ball straight down the middle, a most respectable shot for a man of eighty-four. It had been a full half-century since he won his only Masters title with "the shot heard round the world," a 4-wood that carried the pond on the 15th and skipped into the hole for a double eagle, vaulting Sarazen into a tie for the lead (he won the tournament in a playoff).

Snead, a three-time Masters champion and, at seventy-four, another monument of longevity, took a fluid, handsome swipe at the ball. He once said that he liked his swing to feel "oily," and it still looked well lubricated. Snead's last flourish at Augusta had been back in 1963, when he came very close to proving that a man over fifty could still win the Masters. With only three holes left to play, he was nursing a one-stroke lead; the man who caught him was less than half his age, a twenty-three-year-old named Jack Nicklaus.

Neither of these two venerable campaigners made much headway against par, but then neither did many of the younger men who followed them. The usual first-round jitters had something to do with that—Donnie Hammond, playing in his first Masters, soared to four over par after the first five holes, and "wanted to run and hide behind one of those big pine trees"—but the wind had even more. It gusted up to 25 miles per hour, making the air a living hazard and playing havoc with the high, soft approach shots that most players feel it is essential to hit at Augusta. Moreover, the wind had dried out the greens, and the pins had been placed in such difficult positions that a good many contestants found themselves playing from the fringes all day long. As the numbers began to go up on the scoreboards, it became apparent that on this particular Thursday, birdies would be hard to come by.

Nearly every player in the field was having trouble getting close to the flag, and even more trouble getting the ball into the cup. Long-hitting Fred Couples managed to reach the 555-yard second hole, a par 5, with two good shots; he barely tapped his 10-foot eagle putt and watched—with the fine philosophical indignation that is familiar to all golfers—as the ball rolled a full 40 feet past the hole. He then rammed home his birdie. Roger Maltbie, the popular, rumpled "Rajah," usually half-hidden in a cloud of swirling cigarette smoke, managed to post a 71, and he took four of those strokes with his putter on the 16th green. The apparently ageless Gary Player, competing in his twenty-ninth Masters, suffered the indignity of a four-putt on the ninth green—and the greens at both No. 9 and No. 18 had been rebuilt during the winter to make the slopes less severe.

A word about those immense, weaving greens, which have always been the pride and terror of Augusta National. Originally seeded with thin rye grass, they were converted to Bermuda, the standard grass for Southern courses; but in 1980 they were seeded yet again, this time with bent grass, which can be mowed exceedingly short and which, like the mills of justice, grinds exceedingly fine. When they were unveiled for the 1981 Masters, it was immediately clear that these new bent-grass greens were going to be absolutely unforgiving. Putts that used to break a handspan now broke a foot, and downhill putts—which often as not are sidehill as well—presented roughly the same challenge as putting over the freshly waxed hood of a Porsche, attempting to stop the ball on the bumper. Many a golfer admitted that he was just too spooked by a downhill putt to swing the club—and when a golfer decelerates the blade, he doesn't have a prayer of getting the ball into the hole. Uphill putts weren't quite as dire, but nothing could be taken for granted on the bent grass. There was no such thing as a tap-in, and on putts of medium length, most players tried to make sure that if they missed, they missed on the low side of the hole.

Understandably, the players had grumbled about the greens, and two of the chief villains—No. 9 and No. 18—had been shaved down to make the back-to-front tilt less precipitous. On the whole, however, the bent grass had done exactly what Masters officials hoped; the greens were the great equalizers on a course that is neither fearsomely long nor tight.

One of America's most influential golf course architects, Charles Blair Macdonald, maintained that "putting-greens to a golf course are what the face is to a portrait. The clothes the subject wears, the background, whether scenery or whether draperies—are simply accessories; the face tells the story and determines the quality of the portrait." Applying that standard, you might be tempted to compare the greens of Augusta National to the expression on the Mona Lisa—perfectly composed and utterly enigmatic.

The scores on Thursday ran unusually high. Only fifteen of the eighty-eight contestants broke par, and the stroke average for the field was 75.1, more than three strokes over par. The wind kept right on scouring the greens, and by midday the bent grass had acquired an icy blue sheen around the cups, where players and caddies had been walking. Several golfers who'd come to Augusta with high hopes looked grim and disgruntled when they trudged off the last green, knowing their chances were pretty much scuttled. Hale Irwin shot a 76, and Scott Verplank a 77. Two of the stalwarts of the American tour, Lanny Wadkins (78) and Hal Sutton (80), were going to have to produce a sparkling round just to make the cut. So would that legendary hero Arnold Palmer, who shot an 80 in front of a somewhat diminished but still faithful army.

The highest round of the day, an 82, belonged to Mac O'Grady. He claimed that his dispute with Beman hadn't bothered him; on the contrary, it had "empowered" him, though the power had obviously not manifested itself in his score. The cosmological O'Grady was able to put the treachery of the greens into a higher intellectual context: "There are so many multiple undulations on the greens, Newton's law will certainly be the final force. Newton would be proud of himself here."

O'Grady made the turn in 37, despite three-putting both the 7th and 8th greens. The back nine was when it all started slip-sliding away, and his troubles provide a nice illustration of just how tough the course was playing. At the 10th hole he hit a booming drive and pitched with a 9-iron. The ball spun back against the collar. He read the putt to go left, but it broke right. His par-saver switched out of the hole. Bogey. At No. 12, the tricky par 3 where the tee shot has to carry Rae's Creek and contend with the winds that swirl confusingly off the backdrop of pines, he watched his playing partner, Greg Norman, hit a 7-iron 3 feet from the hole. He also hit a 7-iron, and the ball dropped into the creek. Trying to get a stroke back, he hit a big drive and a 3-wood at No. 13, a 465-yard par 5. The ball bored through the wind, flew safely over the pond, and skittered off the back edge of the green. It was a spot O'Grady could enter on his own personal list of places not to miss a green. He was one of a handful of players who managed to reach the 15th green, the second of the short par 5s on the back nine; both were playing into the wind, and since both greens are protected by water hazards, most players had laid up. O'Grady had a 60-foot putt for his eagle. He left it 8 feet short. "If I hit it a baby's breath harder," he said, "it's perfect. And if I hit it firm, off the front of the green. On my second putt, I played a three-inch break but it broke eighteen inches. Then I missed the next one. Four putts. And when I put it in the water on the sixteenth, I was saying to myself, 'I can't make a par on the back nine.'"

O'Grady did finish the round with two pars, but that 82 meant that he was going to have to tap into all the mystical energies of the game if he wanted to make the cut. He would have done well to meditate on the fortunes of Curtis Strange, the low-key Virginian who opened the 1985 Masters with an 80, made his plane reservations home, and with the freedom of the golfer who has already been blasted by calamity, with no place to go but up, proceeded on Friday to play himself right back into contention with a round of 65. By the time that tournament was over, Strange would take the lead and lose it, an experience that, in O'Grady-ese, must have been something like "going to the mountain and becoming one with the lava."

This year Strange was off to a less harrowing start with a score of 73, and the man who had profited most from his disaster, defending Masters champion Bernhard Langer, opened with a 74. Langer hadn't hit the ball badly, but he simply shrugged and said, "I couldn't handle the greens." He then reported to the putting green to experiment with several new sticks.

Three other Masters champions—Ray Floyd, Craig Stadler, and Jack Nicklaus—were also at 74, and Nicklaus had waged his own inglorious battle on the greens. His tee-to-green game hadn't let him down, but by his own count, he'd had eleven "makable" putts, putts inside 15 feet—and he'd made only one of them. His single birdie of the day came at No. 13. His new oversized putter only made his troubles on the green more conspicuous, and even the most ardent Nicklaus fans, remembering how loyally he had stuck with his old blade, a conventional flange putter, were inclined to look on the new stick as a grasping at straws and further evidence of the Golden Bear's decline. Nicklaus certainly didn't sound likely to threaten anyone when he said, "I'm amazed that the guys are making any putts out there."

What of the other favorites? Ballesteros claimed to be pleased with his game after a safe and steady round of 71. The one shot he would have liked back was the pitching wedge he hit to the 15th green after laying up short of the pond. The ball landed inches short of the green and spun back down the bank of the pond, almost into the water. It took him three to get down from there. "One mental mistake at Augusta is very good," he remarked at the end of the day. "This course will jump up and bite you quick."

Though he came into the tournament only as a sentimental favorite, Ben Crenshaw was also at 71. The sweet-tempered Texan who won the Masters in 1984 had then fallen into a slump that was more like an abyss, plummeting right off the money list. Like most golfers, he thought the troubles were in his head, and he tried to soldier straight through them. He floundered for a year before he finally went to a doctor, who diagnosed a thyroid condition and put him on medication. Now Crenshaw, newly married, had regained most of the weight he'd lost; he was telling people that he was actually playing better than when he won in 1984. Since Crenshaw is one of the best putters in the game, he was very much in the hunt.

In the group a stroke ahead of him, at 70, there were several players who had reason to be happy with their performance. Bob Tway had won his first tournament only a few months before, defeating Bernhard Langer in a playoff at San Diego; now he would get his first taste of competing for a major. Greg Norman, often a slow starter, turned in a workmanlike round that included only one bogey, and emphasized the demands the course made on a player's judgment: "Augusta National is one course where you've got to keep your ego under control." Tom Kite, a perennial contender, had an almost identical card, his lone bogey coming at the first hole. Two of the fifteen international players, Canada's Dave Barr and Japan's Tommy Nakajima, were also at 70.

Tom Watson had hit the ball like 76, but he escaped with a 70, thanks to an eagle on No. 13—he registered the only eagle of the day at that hole—and eight other one-putt greens. The author of an instruction book entitled *Getting Up and Down,* Watson had done some nifty scrambling and deft putting, and this was bad news for his adversaries. Watson can play all the shots, but the heart of his game has always been his dogged refusal to give up strokes. When Watson really gets going, he believes staunchly in his ability to get down from anywhere on or around a green—a conviction that has produced memorable results. For over a year he had looked uncharacteristically tentative, but in his press interview he said of his round, "That's what I've needed to do and haven't been able to do for a long time." He obviously relished the opportunity to answer a question other than the one that had plagued him for over a year now—what's wrong with Tom Watson? As for his swing, he credited a fan with helping him to get back on the right track. "Somebody wrote me a letter and said, 'Go read your own book,' and he was right. You have to make a slow, deliberate change of direction at the top of the backswing."

Watson had to like his position when he looked at the leader board in the interview room. There were only four men ahead of him, none of whom had ever won a major. T. C. Chen, he of double-chip fame, was at 69 after another sort of double-chip had produced a birdie at No. 13. Chen was able to carry Rae's Creek with his second shot at No. 13, but he was in the fringe; he chipped clear over the green into the opposite fringe. From there he chipped again and holed out for his third birdie in a row. He had birdied his way through Amen Corner, and for good measure he tacked on another birdie at No. 14, giving him the lowest score of the day on the back nine, a 32.

The only other golfer at 69 was Gary Koch, the winner of the Par-3 Contest, who kept his hot hand on the short holes. He deuced three of them, No. 6, No. 12, and No. 16, but his fine round was one shy of the lead shared by two little-known American golfers.

Ken Green—the other Green, not Hubert but the bubbly, bespectacled, boyish twenty-eight-year-old from Connecticut who'd earned his Masters invitation by winning the Buick Open—rolled in a 40-footer on the first hole. On the roller coaster fifth green, he holed an even more monstrous putt, a

70-footer. First-timers at the Masters are supposed to be nervous, but Green was obviously enjoying himself and playing to the crowd. "I'm trying to downplay the tournament as much as I can," he said. "If I say, 'God, the Masters,' I'll choke." His sister, Shelley, a "retired" bookkeeper, was caddying for him, her curls tumbling out from beneath the green Masters cap all caddies are required to wear. Her freckle-faced, all-American good looks attracted plenty of notice, and the bag she carried was topped by Paddington Bear wood covers, an appropriate symbol for the Green entourage, which usually includes Ken's son, various cousins, and other family members, as well as two large dogs and a ferret. Green, who is likely to begin an interview by announcing, "I am not a clone," likes to trace his golfing pedigree back to the barnstormers of the 1930s, and he sees himself not just as a golfer but as an entertainer.

He was certainly putting on a show. He birdied No. 16 with a 70-foot "no-brainer," and he polished off the round with one last indecently long putt at No. 18, posting what would stand as the day's low score, a 68. He and Shelley were ushered to the Butler Cabin for a television interview, and then to the press facility, where his opening line was, "I am not an unknown. Everybody in my family knows me." He carried on in the same ebullient vein until Watson was escorted into the room in a convoy of green-coated officials. "Go on, kick me out," Green said. "By now I'm used to being the other Green. I played a practice round with Hubert the other day, and when we got to the ninth green, I heard a fan say, 'Why does Hubert have two caddies?' "

Bill Kratzert, a veteran journeyman with a sound Masters record—his best finish was a tie for 5th in 1978, and in 1985 he closed with a pair of 69s to finish tied for 14th—shared the lead with Green, and he too had tamed the greens. His 68 included only twenty-seven putts. "I just woke up with the delicate touch I needed," he said, but the day before he woke in a very different frame of mind and fired his regular caddy. A friend from Fort Wayne, Indiana, Chuck Hofius, an electronic components salesman, carried his bag for him, and Hofius was on cloud nine. "If we win," he said, "they'll have to tear these [white caddy] coveralls off me."

Kratzert struck a more somber note in his interview. At the age of thirty-three, he had been on the tour for ten years, long enough to taste the highs and lows of a professional golfer's experience. Highly touted as a young player, he won a tournament in each of his first seasons, and twice in his first three years he was in the top ten on the money list. Then he injured his wrist, lost his swing, fell to 166 on the money list— his earnings went below $15,000—and contemplated leaving the tour. "I don't like to look back at what happened to me," he said. "Lord knows how I made it." When Kratzert expressed his heartfelt thanks to the friends who'd stuck by him, it was hard not to reflect on the fine line that separates success from near-success in professional golf, the fine line that so easily widens into a gulf. On the far side of that gulf, Kratzert could appreciate more sharply than anyone exactly what it meant to have the undivided attention of the golfing media and, through the media, of golf fans all over the world.

What would it mean to Bill Kratzert or Ken Green to win the Masters? It would change their lives, of course, and Bobby Jones used to speculate that the pressure of a major championship is too much for all but a handful of the sturdiest competitors. In his opinion, it was actually more difficult to win an ordinary tournament, in which so many talented players were likely to prevail, and the record books certainly bear him out. A few Masters winners have come out of relative obscurity, but a very few; the hard fact of the matter was that not many people gave Bill Kratzert or Ken Green much of a chance to stave off the powerhouse golfers bunched right behind them.

**THE LEADERS AFTER 18 HOLES**

| | |
|---|---|
| Bill Kratzert | 68 |
| Ken Green | 68 |
| Gary Koch | 69 |
| T. C. Chen | 69 |
| Dave Barr | 70 |
| Tommy Nakajima | 70 |
| Bob Tway | 70 |
| Tom Watson | 70 |
| Greg Norman | 70 |
| Tom Kite | 70 |

# 4

# Friday

"There are two kinds of golf," wrote Bobby Jones, who had some experience in these matters, "golf—and tournament golf. And they are not at all the same thing."

Golf, ordinary golf, was a wonderful way to spend a Sunday afternoon, but tournament golf—even though Jones made it look like a stroll in the park—was a test of a man's nerves and endurance. Though outwardly cool and composed, Jones was inwardly ablaze when competing for a title, and the fire burned hottest in a major championship. Jones was so keyed up that he could hardly eat before he teed off, and after one tournament round he had to ask O. B. Keeler, his devoted Boswell, to unknot his sweaty necktie: his own shaking hands weren't equal to the task. During the 1919 U.S. Amateur, playing a weeklong series of 36-hole matches, Jones lost eighteen pounds, not from the physical strain but from the "nerve-tension." Medal play was just as grueling, for it wasn't a man of flesh and blood you were pitted against, a man who might make a mistake at any moment, but something more abstract and inexorable. In medal play the opponent was an "iron score," and what bore down on you, hole by hole and shot by shot, was the "iron certitude" of knowing that the smallest error could scuttle your chances.

Today's players do not use phrases like "iron certitude," but they do talk about the "mental grind," which comes to much the same thing. It is the player who can stand up to four days of steadily rising pressure without making an error, at least not a disastrous error, who prevails at the end. Golf tournaments are often compared to horse races or to examinations, but the tournament golfer also has something in common with the climber making his slow, painstaking way up the sheer face of a mountain: He can't let down his guard for a single moment. His judgment is critical, and it comes into play every time he makes a move—and every movement must be precisely executed. At any point along the route, the smallest slip can be fatal, but the higher he climbs, the harder it is to keep his wits about him.

The players who teed off first on Friday morning were those with the highest scores, and they were hanging on by their fingernails. They knew they'd have to carve out a better round today if they wanted to make the cut, which is always set 10 strokes above the leader's 36-hole total. It was not going to be easy. The greens were still fast as mercury, several pins were in diabolical locations, and the same southwest wind was popping the flags atop the main scoreboard. The wind wasn't quite as brisk as it had been yesterday, but it was still chiseling away at the already tiny margin for error.

By early afternoon, when the big guns were just going off, the dew-sweepers were already completing their rounds. Most scores were still running well above par, but a few players managed to come back from the brink. Two who'd started poorly, Nick Price and John Mahaffey, knocked 10 strokes from their opening round, going from 79 to 69. It was still too early to predict exactly where the cut would fall, but with a total of 148, Price and Mahaffey were probably safe. Jay Haas rebounded from a 76 to a 69. Mac O'Grady had redeemed his pride with a 70, but only his pride; his two-round total of 152 wasn't likely to see him into the final rounds. Another player who gained ground dramatically was Mark McCumber, a short, stocky strongman who has won four titles on the tour, including two Doral Opens. A former student for the ministry, McCumber is both a perfectionist and a constant seether, a golfer who could honestly say, "I never hit a shot I really liked." Nevertheless, McCumber had agonized his way from a 76 to a 67, and he would win a crystal vase for the day's low score.

So the leaders knew that Augusta National wasn't quite as flinty an adversary as it had been on Thursday, and the scoreboards soon began to show that a battle royal was under way. Looking at the gilt-edged names bunched together at the top, and listening to the cheers that were beginning to erupt from all corners of the course, one veteran Masters watcher remarked that the excitement made this feel more like the third round of the tournament than the second. Ballesteros was making a move, and Langer had got himself right back into the thick of the fray. Chen, Kratzert, Nakajima, and Crenshaw were hanging on gamely. Two other contenders, Greg Norman and Tom Watson, were paired in the day's most glamorous twosome, and when they made the turn—Norman in 34, Watson in 35—they had one of the largest galleries in tow.

The two men were at very different points in their career, a difference that could be exactly measured by using Winged Foot as a reference point. It was there, in the 1974 U.S. Open, that Watson, after leading much of the way, staggered home with a six-over-par 41 on the back nine of the final round and got tagged as a choker. It is easier for a camel to pass through the eye of a needle than for a golfer to shake a reputation for choking, but Watson did it. He won the British Open in 1975, and when he staved off a Nicklaus charge in the 1977 Masters, he removed all doubts about whether he had the right stuff. After that, of course, Watson regularly came up with clutch shots when he needed them and especially when he was up against archrival Nicklaus.

Watson's sangfroid was a matter of record, but Norman's was still in doubt. He had played a wild and woolly last round at Winged Foot when the Open returned there in 1984, spraying the ball all over the place but saving three believe-it-or-not pars on the last three holes to force a playoff with Fuzzy Zoeller. When he dropped his last astounding putt, after his approach had zoomed off toward the gallery, Zoeller, standing in the 18th fairway, waved the white towel—prematurely, as it turned out. Norman had used up all his miracles, and lost the 18-hole playoff by eight strokes.

That defeat might have demoralized another golfer, but Norman is not one to mope. Only two weeks earlier he had won the Kemper Open, his first victory on the American tour, and he took his showing at Winged Foot as a sign that he could hold his own in a big event. He was off on a spree. Over the course of the next few weeks he tied for 10th at Atlanta, won the Canadian Open, finished 2d at the Western Open—he lost a playoff to Tom Watson—and tied for 6th at the British Open. Not bad, but the connoisseurs of choke pointed out that Norman could have won four tournaments during that stretch, and that his playoff record was now 0–3 (his first playoff loss came in 1983, when he made up six strokes on Mike Nicolette in the Bay Hill Classic, only to lose the playoff with a bogey on the first extra hole). When Norman had an off season in 1985, and failed to defend his Canadian Open title after sprinting to a three-stroke lead—he closed with a pair of 73s—he was beginning to look not only like a choker but like a flash in the pan. One last blot on his record had come here at Augusta, during the 1981 Masters, when he took himself out of contention with a double bogey during the final round. The knock on Greg Norman was that he couldn't hold on at the end.

Norman, of course, was keenly aware of the great expectations—and the nagging doubts—that had grown up around him. Here was a man who looked, as Dan Jenkins said, "like the guy you send out to get double-o-seven." He had the most macho of macho nicknames, he oozed confidence, he was the longest, straightest hitter in the game. Obviously relishing his celebrity, he regaled the press with tall tales about the land down under and publicly set outrageously high goals for himself. He posed in a bikini for a golf magazine, and he talked breezily about the possibility of breaking 60. His taste for fast cars, for speed and thrills of all kinds, was well publicized. This Shark had pearly teeth, but some of them were false—he knocked out his own when he fell while being towed by a powerboat. Not long before this Masters, he told an interviewer that he was pointing toward two tournaments in 1986, one in April and the other in July. He didn't have to say that these were the Masters and the British Open. Greg Norman, in short, had the looks, the flair, and the image of a world-beater—but he didn't yet have the credentials.

When he arrived in Augusta, he declared that his game was "on a rise, not a wane." Four weeks earlier in New Orleans, after barely surviving the 36-hole cut, Norman had entered the Sunday round far back in the pack, 18 strokes behind the leader. It was a position he'd been in more often than he liked. That Sunday he shot a good, tight 67, and felt his game starting to click together. He was trying to overcome more than a slump; for the last fifteen months he'd been fighting a mysterious respiratory ailment, playing with a nasty cough, raging temperatures, wooziness, and dysentery. The ailment seemed to be a stubborn case of walking pneumonia, but one doctor had diagnosed an allergy to grass. "It could be worse," Norman said. "I could be allergic to beer." Privately, though, he and his wife, Laura, had been worried that he might have lung tumors or even lung cancer. When the illness was finally diagnosed as a bronchial infection and treated with antibiotics, he felt as if a great weight had been lifted from him, and he arrived at the Masters fit and ready to play.

Through 27 holes Norman had been cruising along nicely. When he reached the 10th hole, he was two under par for the day, four under for the tournament, and tied with Ballesteros for the lead. His round was bogey-free. In fact, his only bogey of the entire tournament had come at the 1st hole on Thursday. He was playing judicious golf, keeping his "ego under control," just as he had promised himself. Now, as he stood on the tee and surveyed the acres of green lying beneath him, he tried once more to rein himself in, for the tee shot at No. 10 is one of the most enticing in the world. The luxuriant fairway tumbles down a long, undulating slope toward a huge Rorschach bunker and a shadow-streaked green some 485 yards from the tee. Because of the descent the hole plays shorter than that, but 485 yards is still a long, long way. On the right side of the fairway, under pines a hundred feet tall and a hundred years old, there is a bargeload of pink azaleas; those towering pines encircle the green, and the light sieves down through the needles as if in a vast cathedral. The pines rise high on the opposite side of the fairway, too, adding their grandeur to the scene.

The scale of this 10th hole is heroic, and the tee shot tempts a golfer like Greg Norman to cut loose. Not only is it downhill, but if he can just turn the ball over and draw it close to the pines on the left—the hole bends gently to the left, more like a bow than a dogleg—he can drive the ball 300 yards, or even 350 yards. (Tom Weiskopf once blasted a drive all the way into that bunker nearly 400 yards away. Nobody had ever been in it before; the bunker marks the spot where the green used to sit before the hole was lengthened, and nobody was ever *supposed* to be in it.)

The sand glistens in the distance, an inviting target—but Norman wisely refused the challenge. This was the hole and this was the selfsame tee shot that had ruined him in 1981. He had come to this tee with a very real chance to win the Masters, unloaded on the ball, hooked it into the timber, and come away with a double bogey 6. Instead of winning the tournament, he'd finished fourth.

So this time, Norman gave the pines a wide berth, playing the hole to par it. His long approach finished against the fringe at the back left of the green, maybe 40 feet from the hole. His par seemed to be in the bag. He had played the hole prudently—but Greg Norman is not the kind of golfer who can tolerate much prudence. When things are going too smoothly, a small voice seems to whisper in his ear the words of the poet William Blake: "Prudence is a rich, ugly, old maid courted by Incapacity." Words to that effect, anyway.

Norman's instinct is to create excitement, and that is exactly what he did. He ran his approach putt a good 12 feet past the hole. If he was bored when he hit that putt, the next one, his par-saver, had his full attention. He was still away, and he was steaming as he studied the line. He was not thinking three-putt; he was all grimness and glare as he took his stance—an open, upright stance, right hand on the putter, left palm on his hip as he lined the ball up on the toe of his putter—and he looked as if he might drill a hole with his eyes if the ball didn't happen to fall into the hole already provided. It didn't. It ghosted 4 feet past the hole, and Norman *still* had a tough putt. No one in the gallery dared to laugh when it, too, switched out of the cup, leaving him with a 2-footer that was by no means a gimme. Has anyone ever *five*-putted? Norman didn't, but he said afterward, "I could still be out there putting that S-O-B." He had taken the most ignominious kind of double bogey and provided a perfect object lesson of what Bobby Jones called "the fatal mistake of playing safe."

Exit the Shark, wrathfully. He didn't simmer down until he had lost another stroke at No. 11, where a loose approach finished yards wide of the green. He'd frittered away three strokes, and given himself no choice but to attack. He birdied the 15th when he got down with a chip and a putt, and at No. 16, where the pin was cut on a little plateau at the back right of the green—the most difficult pin position at this 170-yard par 3—he came through with a superlative shot. One player after another, fearing the bunker just behind the flag, had left the approach short, only to watch his ball roll well back toward the pond. Norman fired off a high 6-iron that covered the pin all the way and sizzled to a halt a foot from the hole. When he bogeyed the 18th to finish with a 72, he had to be kicking himself. Every golfer writes his own script during a tournament, and Norman's script—if he was to get back into the lead—now cried out for a melodramatic turnabout. Norman was typecast for the role.

Back to Tom Watson. He really tagged his drive at No. 10, and as he swung down the fairway after planting a crisp approach shot exactly where he wanted it—about 10 feet below the hole—he seemed to be hitting his stride. Radiating some of the jaunty confidence of the Watson of old, he actually accelerated when he reached the slope leading up to the 10th green, almost running the last few steps to get a close look at his birdie putt. He has the heads-up, alert quality of a point guard in basketball pushing the ball upcourt, looking for that little opening, the one tiny crack he needs to drive the lane and stuff the ball. It is that *push* that marked Watson's play from 1977 to 1984, his glory years; he looked as if he couldn't wait to get to the green and knock the ball into the hole.

Whether Watson meant to intimidate his opponents with his try-and-stop-me attitude, or whether it was simply his own way of stoking the inner fires, the effect was certainly intimidating. Norman, for one, remarked that Watson just "looked right through you," and even Ballesteros once admitted that sometimes, against Watson, he felt the heat. Watson didn't seem to see anything but the ball and the cup, and he was a terror around the greens. The big hitters have a psychological edge because of their length; Walter Hagen, when he was on his irons, used to let himself be outdriven so that he could stick the ball close to the flag, wearing down his opponents by being inside them hole after hole. Watson's style was to hole out from all over the place. Just when he seemed to have lost a stroke, he curled in an impossible putt, or even worse, a chip. For a decade he had probably been the best putter and the most feared scrambler in golf. Just before that lob-chip that won the U.S. Open at Pebble Beach, his caddy said, "Get it close." Without missing a beat, Watson replied, "I'm not gonna get it close, I'm gonna make it."

That, of course, is the deep, unshakable confidence that wins golf tournaments and rattles the competition, and Watson used to bristle with it, especially on the greens. Now, though, after watching Norman miss the cup with two slap shots, Watson stepped warily up to his birdie putt. He'd had plenty of time to survey the putt, and he wanted still further appraisal—though he once would have trusted his first keen impression. He finally took his stance. In countless interviews over the last two years he had been asked what was wrong with his putting, and his stock reply was "I just can't get comfortable over the ball." He did not look comfortable now. He looked instead like a man who has just dropped his ring down a drain and is trying, to no avail, to coax it out with a coat hanger. His shoulders were high and stiff, his arms were pressed against his sides, and his hands looked tense and rigid on the grip. Still, the ball fell in for a birdie, and Watson was within a stroke of the lead.

One of the oldest maxims in golf is to play one shot at a time, but it must have been hard for Watson to keep his mind from racing ahead. He was two under par for the day, three under for the tournament, and he'd just birdied one of the toughest holes on the course. With the rest of the back nine to play—and the back is considered the more forgiving of the nines, with those two short par 5s—a 69, or even a 68, was a real possibility. He could almost count on being in pursuit at the end of his round, and he knew that the man he was pursuing was Ballesteros. A few years earlier, when Watson was at the top of his game, he had said that he welcomed the challenge from Ballesteros; but with the exception of the British Open at St. Andrews, the two had never gone head-to-head in the last round of a major championship. It was too early to imagine that they'd be the last ones left in this Masters, but it was gratifying to Watson, after his lean years, to be back at center stage.

Whatever Watson was thinking, it didn't help his drive at No. 11. The ball was in the fairway, but it barely cleared the broad, low crest about 210 yards from the tee. This par 4 is 455 yards long, and Watson was a good 225 yards from the flag, looking at an approach shot that would make anyone gulp. He selected a 2-iron, and he would need all of it. The wind was in his face and blowing from his right, toward the kidney-shaped pond that guards the entire left front of the green. There's plenty of trouble behind the green—Rae's Creek is back there, with two bunkers thrown in for good measure—but the pond is the hazard that puts the lump in the throat. Ben Hogan hated that pond. He once said, "If you see me on that green with my second shot, you'll know I missed it." He always aimed his approach toward the safe right edge of the green, and the way Watson set up to play his shot, it looked as if he wanted to make sure that he was to the right.

Watson hit exactly the kind of shot he had been dreading, a duck hook that darted so far to the left that he missed the pond and found the creek behind it. He had closed his clubface at the top of his backswing, the very fault he had worked so assiduously to correct on the practice tee. He had to drop on the far side of the pond, and he was lucky to save his bogey by sliding in a 12-footer.

Trouble often comes like grapes, in bunches, and Watson made another error at the short 12th, this time an error in judgment. Depending on the wind and the pin placement, the tee shot on this par 3 can require anything from a 9-iron to a 5-iron. Today the pin was cut directly behind the bunker which noses up the short, steep bank that rises from the water, and the wind was roiling high in the pines, full of currents and eddies. Watson misread it. He hit a high 7-iron that drifted to his left and splashed down in the pond.

The gallery—and the gallery included not only those fans who were following him and Norman but the thousands of spectators taking in the action at Amen Corner—was shocked. There were gasps and groans and all kinds of speculations. Watson had now hit three bad shots in a row, and minutes later, from the drop area, he hit a fourth, a pitch that failed to clear the bunker. He did well to get down in two and escape with a triple bogey. Why hadn't he played a safer shot from the tee? Ballesteros had punched his shot here, making sure he carried the water, refusing to traffic with the wind. Had Watson been too eager to make up the stroke he lost at the 11th? On the last round, perhaps, if he came to No. 12 two strokes behind the leader, Watson would have had no choice but to attack the flag—but on the second round? When the penalty for failing to bring off the shot was so extreme, what had possessed Watson to attempt it?

Watson finished out his round with a birdie at No. 13 and a three-putt bogey at No. 16, giving him a 74 for the day and a two-round total of 144. Nobody was ready to count him out, but you don't win major championships with triple bogies on your card, and Watson's fans were dissecting his round with melancholy fascination. In one of the lounges in the press room, a writer asked, "Tom Watson? The guy with the fast backswing? Used to win a lot of tournaments? What's wrong with him, anyway?" That was the question that had already plagued Watson for months, and it looked as though he would have to go right on answering it.

* * *

Watson wasn't the only American golfer who had a bad day. When the pollen finally settled and the numbers were all totted up, it was clear that the foreign invasion everybody had been buzzing about was taking place. Five of the top eight spots on the scoreboard were occupied by foreign players, and the leader of the assault, to no one's surprise, was Seve Balles-teros. On a day when most of the field had struggled, he had put together a round of 68, giving him a two-day total of 139 and a one-stroke lead.

Bill Kratzert was in second place at 140, and Tommy Nakajima was in sole possession of third place at 141. Greg Norman, T. C. Chen, and Bernhard Langer were tied at 142 with two Americans, Ben Crenshaw and Danny Edwards, each of whom had shot back-to-back 71s. Several talented younger players—Mark McCumber, Corey Pavin, and Bob Tway— were right behind them, but a good many of the mainstays of the tour had faltered.

Tom Kite had slipped from 70 to 74, and Roger Maltbie (71–75), Hubert Green (71–75), and Gary Koch (69–74) had all backed up, but not as drastically as Ken Green. "I played hockey out there," he said, and that was as good a description as any of his round of 78. His only moment of glory came at No. 18, where he knocked a blind explosion shot into the cup for a birdie. Green had no idea that the ball was anywhere near the pin, but when he heard the cheers, he raised his arms like Rocky Balboa and sashayed out of the bunker as if he'd just won the tournament.

Bill Kratzert didn't have much to crow about, either, though he was the leading American player after a hard-work-ing round of 72. His putter hadn't exactly let him down, but yesterday's magic was gone. "I shot about what I should have shot. I don't think I could have gotten any more out of it," Kratzert said, summing up a card that showed three birdies and three bogeys.

Three American golfers who had loomed large in the early handicapping—Andy Bean, Hal Sutton, and Craig Stadler—

had missed the cut. So did Ray Floyd, who burned up the course when he won the Masters in 1976. His 36-hole total that year was 131, a record that still stands, and 21 strokes better than his performance this year. Gary Player, at 150, must have winced when Ballesteros, an old friend, poured in a birdie putt at No. 18, lowering the cutoff to 149 (the field for the last two rounds is always composed of golfers within 10 strokes of the leader). This would be only the third time in his twenty-nine Masters appearances that Player failed to complete the tournament. Arnold Palmer, in his thirty-second consecutive Masters, missed his seventh cut.

Jack Nicklaus, one of the oldest competitors left in the field, was the youngest member of the Big Three, the triumvirate of Palmer, Player, and Nicklaus that had ruled the Masters. In the eight years between 1958 and 1966, they accounted for seven Masters victories, and in the twenty-year span from 1958 to 1978, they won an even dozen Masters. Player was the last to win, in 1978, when he shot a sensational 64, taking only 30 shots on the back nine to come from 7 strokes behind. Nicklaus had posted the last of his five Masters victories in 1975. Twice since then he had been the runner-up, but it was looking very much as if a generation had had its last hurrah.

With a 71 after his opening 74, Nicklaus was moving in the right direction, and he was within shouting distance of Ballesteros—but it would have to be a very loud shout. He was still struggling with the oversized putter. Twelve times he'd had birdie putts within 15 feet, but he'd made only three of them. He summed up his performance bluntly, "I've just played my best two rounds of the year, and I haven't scored."

But he hadn't lost faith in the putter. He was having trouble obeying one of the oldest and most fundamental rules in golf: *Keep your head still.* Jack Grout, Nicklaus's earliest teacher, used to hold his star pupil's hair throughout the swing to make sure that the importance of this rule would sink in. Here in Augusta Nicklaus was hitting his full shots as well as he ever had, but somehow he'd fallen into the habit of moving his head when he putted. His wife, Barbara, had noticed this during the practice days, and out on the course, before every putt, Jackie reminded him, "Keep your head still." He was trying to, but the putts still weren't falling.

If the Big Three were the ghosts of Masters Past, the spirits of Masters Present were Bernhard Langer and Seve Ballesteros, who already seemed to be working on a tradition of their own. In the six tournaments since 1980, they had three Masters wins between them. Langer, of course, was the defending champion, and in 1985 Ballesteros had finished right behind him in a three-way tie for second.

They had long since established their preeminence in Europe, though Ballesteros, in large part because of his performances at Augusta, was far better known in the United States. Langer had played infrequently on this side of the Atlantic, but in 1984, on his first extended American swing, he won over $80,000 in eight events, more than enough to qualify him for membership on the American tour. The next year he entered sixteen American tournaments, won two of them, and increased his earnings by almost $200,000—and that was only in this country. Early in the season he won the Australian Masters, and in midsummer, back home in Europe, he lost the Irish Open in a playoff with Ballesteros, finished third in the British Open and second in the Dutch Open, and then won back-to-back victories in the German Open and the European Open. To cap off the season, he traveled to South Africa in December and won the Sun City Open, bringing his year's earnings to over $850,000.

With six tournament victories on four different continents, Langer could have taken as his motto, "Have Clubs, Will Travel." There have been other itinerant golfers from countries that have only the beginnings of a golfing tradition—Gary Player and Roberto de Vicenzo fit the description—but Langer was in the forefront of a new generation of world travelers. Like Ballesteros, he had obviously been steeled by his experience on what amounts to a world tour. Even though his record suggests, and Langer freely admits, that the other circuits can't compare with the American tour in depth of talent, the fact that he had been able to contend on an almost weekly basis had surely helped him to develop a winning attitude.

All the young foreign players vying for the lead in this Masters had impressive win totals. Langer had won twenty-two professional tournaments around the world, Ballesteros forty-four, Norman thirty-three, and Tommy Nakajima thirty. The only American golfers with comparable records were veterans like Tom Watson, who had won thirty-one tournaments in the United States, and six elsewhere—five British Opens and the Dunlop Phoenix in Japan. But Watson was thirty-six years old, and all four foreign golfers were within a year or two of thirty, just entering their prime. Their American contemporaries were players like Mark O'Meara, who could point to three tour wins, Hal Sutton, five, and Curtis Strange, eight. There is no way of knowing exactly what toll it takes on the psyche to compete for a year or two without winning, without even getting into serious contention, but that is the experience of a good many American professionals, even the best ones. It has to be discouraging. It has to affect a player when he finally does get into a position to win. A Ballesteros or a Norman can say to himself, "I've been in this position before. I know how to handle it."

In any event, Langer had turned in a sterling round, 36–32—68. Rifling his iron shots, he was able to keep them low and out of the wind. Three of his five birdies came on the short holes. Langer was also lucky. He had switched to a new putter for Friday's round, and—like Kratzert and Green on Thursday—he was homed in. He ran home a 50-foot birdie putt on the 10th and when another 50-footer dropped at the 16th, he slowly keeled over backward, high histrionics for a man who usually looks as if he just bit into a lemon. At No. 18, where he made a last birdie after his drive found the fairway bunker, he actually kissed his ball after removing it from the cup.

One man who welcomed the wind was Tommy Nakajima. In fact, he would have been quite happy to play in a hurricane; the harder it blows, the more he likes it. His father was a martinet who rigged up an outdoor shower and a huge fan in the garden so that young Tommy could practice in a sort of banzai tempest. The elder Nakajima also installed a tee that could be adjusted to create hilly lies; and to develop his son's strength and stamina, he sent him out to run in the hills dragging a tire along behind him. Not surprisingly, Nakajima rebelled against this training regimen and ran away from home more than once.

Yet he quickly developed into one of Japan's finest young golfers and eventually succeeded Isao Aoki as the top player in Japan. In 1985 he won five tournaments in Japan, and he was listed in fourth place in the SONY World Rankings, behind three European players and ahead of all Americans. Despite his impressive credentials, Nakajima has not fared very well in the United States, his best-ever finish a fourth at Greensboro in 1983. "At home he is expected to win," his interpreter told me, "and when he does win, he is only relieved. But here in America, he wants to win."

Nakajima carried the burden of a nation's ambitions. He was well aware that millions of his fellow countrymen stayed awake into the wee hours of the night to watch the live Masters telecasts, and that the sizable Japanese press contingent followed his every move. Dozens of Nikons whirred every time he swung. Once and sometimes twice a day, he held his own press conference at Augusta, enthroned on his turquoise and white bag just at the edge of the practice green, with members of the Japanese press corps crouched before him. A marked, even reverential formality prevailed, and Nakajima answered each question with senatorial gravity, as befits a national figure. Although golf is relatively new to Japan, and a single round can be fabulously expensive, the Japanese have embraced the game with passion. "We are very competitive," volunteered his young Japanese interpreter. "We sometimes win in business, and we would like to win in golf, too."

To Western eyes, Nakajima hardly has the appearance of a rugged campaigner. His glasses make him look deceptively mild-mannered, and he is always immaculately groomed and dressed. Although he is a six-footer, and considers the long clubs the strength of his game—"I think I am just a little longer," he says, holding up his thumb and forefinger to show a tiny gap, "just a little longer than most players"—he is slender and sleek muscled, not at all brawny. On the practice green at Augusta, he often seemed to drift off in some pleasant contemplation—of a plum blossom, perhaps, or a Kenny Loggins song, for he is a lover of music, and his tastes extend to American rock—forgetting the putter in his hand and the balls at his feet, dreamily batting them back and forth, calling upon his reserves of patience and composure.

He has needed them at the Masters, where he is best remembered for his octuple bogey, the 13 he once scored on the 13th hole. How does a world-class golfer score a 13? Tom Weiskopf, who shares the Masters record for the highest score on a single hole, did it by knocking five balls into Rae's Creek at No. 12. Nakajima, too, hit a shot into the creek, his second shot after an errant drive, and waded in to play the ball out of the water. The ball did squirt out, but not far enough. It rolled back and hit him in the foot—a two-stroke penalty. A moment later, his caddy dropped the club Nakajima was handing him, thus grounding it in the hazard, and he was penalized two strokes more. He was then lying eight and still in the creek. He dropped out, and the last four strokes were a pitch, a chip, and two putts.

Nakajima had borne this misfortune with Job-like fatalism, and now, in this windy Masters, he had done himself proud with solid rounds of 70 and 71. Especially satisfying was the way he'd tamed the 13th, "my old friend." On Thursday he birdied the 13th, and on Friday he was one of only two players to eagle it. Then, with the wind in his face, he was tempted to carry the pond at the 15th. The ball landed on the bank short of the green and rolled back into the water. Nakajima took a bogey, but he finished par, birdie, birdie, leaving him at 141, only two strokes astern of Ballesteros.

The Spaniard had played the most significant round of the day. On the second hole, the longest par 5 at Augusta National, he absolutely blasted the ball off the tee, socking it 365 yards and leaving himself a 6-iron—a 6-iron—to the green. There was a quartering wind to help him, and the fairway runs down-hill, but 365 yards is still a Herculean clout. He two-putted for his birdie, and proceeded to make the front nine look easy. At the 180-yard sixth, he threw up a high, soft 7-iron that coasted on the wind and came in big as a grapefruit. At the seventh, a drive-and-pitch of 360 yards, he drove with a 2-iron and tossed up a sand wedge that sat down only 10 feet from the hole. He should have birdied the eighth, for he reached the green in two, but he three-putted and had to be content with a par.

The other low rounds had been fashioned with the putter, but Ballesteros, using every stick in the bag, was simply swarm-ing along, soliloquizing in Spanish. Other players may weigh all the same considerations that he does, but they do so in silence. He kept up a nonstop rat-a-tat-tat, presumably aimed at Vicente, though Vicente did not often talk back. Ballesteros says that the talking is a way to help him concentrate, and you cannot listen to him, and watch him play, without believing that it works and without suspecting that Ballesteros somehow sees things out on the course that aren't visible to ordinary golfers. Hogan used to say that golf is a game of infinite adjust-ments, that no two shots are ever precisely the same, but Ballesteros is the one present-day golfer who seems to live by this observation. Other golfers try to hit every shot the same way; Ballesteros tries to create the shot, the ideal shot, for the situation. At the 13th, for instance, after he had pushed his drive into the trees—it was his first errant drive of the day—he tried to pull off what would have been a stupendous shot. He had a patchy lie in the rough, only a few yards behind a fat pine tree, but he decided to cut a 3-wood around the tree, to a green 230 yards away and sitting snugly behind a creek. Stupendous? It was an impossible shot, and even Ballesteros couldn't make it. He topped it cold, and the ball went scooting along into the creek, costing him his first bogey of the day.

He was able to offset that bogey at the 15th, when he powered his tee shot into the wind, got home with a 4-wood, and rolled in his 25-foot putt for an eagle. When that putt fell,

Ballesteros, in black and white—black trousers, black sweater, white shoes, white visor—drew himself erect and thrust both arms high into the air, knowing that he had just taken command of the tournament.

He finished the round by rolling in another 25-footer for a birdie at the 18th, making up for a stroke he'd given away at the 16th, where he was bunkered after his tee shot. He had brought in a bold, brassy 68 for a total of 139.

His day's work was not yet done. Minutes after checking his scorecard, Ballesteros was seated in front of the television cameras in Butler Cabin, fielding a question from Brent Musburger, who opened the interview with a flurry of praise, or what sounded like praise. "You came in confident," Musburger said. "You said this was your Masters, you charged right to the top. How do you feel after two rounds?"

"First of all, I must clarify one thing," Ballesteros said evenly. He knew that Musburger was inviting him to predict his own victory; he also knew that the predictions he'd already made had touched off a minor furor. Over the last few days he'd been scolded in print and on the air for his vanity and arrogance—one CBS commentator had called him "foolhardy"—and the criticism had stung. Right now, though, the glow of his fine round was still upon him, and he wanted to explain himself. "I never say this is my Masters. I say I come to Augusta to win, like everybody else. The media people, sometimes they write things the wrong way. So I must clarify that."

Musburger couldn't contain his surprise and gratification, and he looked like a guppy in a feeding frenzy when he asked his next questions. Was Ballesteros denying his prediction? Was he saying the press had exaggerated? What, exactly, had he told the press?

"They were asking me what had been going on with Deane Beman, and I say I come to Augusta to enjoy this place and win the Masters. That don't mean it's my Masters. You can say that only after you won on Sunday."

That was certainly clear enough. With a blithe shrug and

a roguish smile, Ballesteros appeared to dismiss the whole incident. He laughed at the worst stroke he had played during the round, the rabbity 3-wood he hit out of the rough at the 13th—"that ball take off running all over the fairway and into the crick"—and when Musburger asked if his animated conversations with his brother Vicente were arguments, he poked fun at his own temper. "You know the Spanish. We always have hot blood."

Ballesteros, in short, was relaxed and comfortable, and his next stop was the interview room in the press facility where, speaking into the microphones, he described his round for the hundreds of correspondents from all over the globe. He is an old hand at these debriefings, of course, and his English is more than equal to the task. One Spanish writer, Nuria Pastor, who has followed Ballesteros from the beginning of his career, thinks that he is actually more at ease with the English-speaking press than he is in his own country. The British writers who cover the European tour are not only knowledgeable, but they treat him like a golfer. They understand the game, while the Spanish media tend to regard him as something of a curiosity, an athlete who has made his mark in a sport that is still regarded mostly as the pastime of foreigners on holiday.

This press conference purred along smoothly enough at first. Ballesteros went through a blow-by-blow description of his round, allowing that the key to it had been his ability to keep his approach shots below the hole. Through the first 12 holes he had played consistently—"nothing dynamic, but always in good position." He claimed that he hadn't looked at the scoreboard until he finished off the round with that birdie at the 18th. And how did it look then? Ballesteros glanced at the small leader board at one side of the room, with his name at the top of it. He poked his tongue in his cheek and flashed a smile. "Pretty good," he said.

What did he think about the number of foreign players in contention? Were the foreigners the best in the world? Earlier in the week Ballesteros had ruffled some feathers by naming several players who he thought should have been invited to the Masters, but now he ducked the issue. Maybe the foreign-

ers weren't the best players. Maybe they "just scored the best."
He was playing cat and mouse, but he wasn't going to get off
so easily.

When the inevitable questions about Deane Beman were
asked, Ballesteros used his standard quip, "I don't have a problem with Deane Beman, but I think he has a problem with
me."

"You played like you were on a crusade today," one writer
said. "Are you trying to prove something to the PGA Tour?"

"Does Deane Beman pay you to ask me that question
every day?" Ballesteros parried.

"It's a legitimate question."

"You talk too sophisticated for me," he said, and his good
humor was suddenly gone. The interview soon came to an end,
and I asked Nuria what Ballesteros thought of the American
press. She said, "He thinks they don't want him to win."

**THE LEADERS AFTER 36 HOLES**

| | | | |
|---|---|---|---|
| Seve Ballesteros | 71 | 68 | 139 |
| Bill Kratzert | 68 | 72 | 140 |
| Tommy Nakajima | 70 | 71 | 141 |
| Bernhard Langer | 74 | 68 | 142 |
| Danny Edwards | 71 | 71 | 142 |
| Ben Crenshaw | 71 | 71 | 142 |
| Greg Norman | 70 | 72 | 142 |
| T. C. Chen | 69 | 73 | 142 |
| Mark McCumber | 76 | 67 | 143 |
| Corey Pavin | 71 | 72 | 143 |
| Bob Tway | 70 | 73 | 143 |
| Gary Koch | 69 | 74 | 143 |

# 5

# Seve Agonistes

The career of Severiano Ballesteros got underway like a Grand Prix race, with roaring noises, high combustion, and blazing speed.

Before the 1976 British Open at Royal Birkdale, he was an obscure, untested, ridiculously young professional (he was only 19) from Spain, of all places. The most significant title he had won was the Under-25 Championship for Spanish professionals. He was a reckless golfer with a long, lashing swing, and his only strategy was to attack—and if he missed his target, to regroup and attack again. Inevitably, because he was Spanish, he would often be compared to a matador, but at Birkdale he bore a greater resemblance to a fierce young fighting bull. He tore into every drive and played the Open from all over the course, taking the shaggy dunes in stride and barging through the knee-high rough. At the end of each of the first three days, he was leading the British Open.

He took a two-stroke lead into the final round, and at last did what an inexperienced golfer is expected to do under those circumstances: he faltered. Paired with Johnny Miller, the eventual winner, he had fallen back into a tie by the 6th hole, and the strokes kept dropping away. Miller, playing a steady and circumspect brand of golf, was out of reach by the time they had finished 12 holes, but Ballesteros was determined to salvage what he could. With a pair of birdies and an eagle in the home stretch, he picked up four strokes, and he came to the finishing hole needing a par to tie for third, a birdie to tie for second.

The 18th at Royal Birkdale is a 513-yard par 5. Ballesteros didn't quite get home in two. His approach was left of the green and short, and the ball came to rest in a scrubby patch of rough. The green was only 20 yards away, but a pair of bunkers, separated by a narrow path, intervened. The pin was 6 or 7 yards behind the bunkers, and the wind was behind Ballesteros. If he tried to pitch over the bunkers, from that lie to that pin placement on a glassy green, he judged that he would probably run the ball too far past the hole to give himself a chance for the birdie he wanted. He took a closer look at the path between the bunkers. It was hard, humped, and only two feet wide, but if he could pitch onto it with a low 9-iron, keeping the ball under the wind, and if the ball bounced just below the crest—well, it would hop onto the green and expire near the cup.

Which, of course, is exactly what happened. He brought off an unforgettable shot, one that combined sheer audacity with supreme finesse. Ballesteros would come to consider it the most important shot of his early career, the shot that launched him. To himself, and to the world, he'd served notice that he would refuse to be daunted by the pressure of a big event. The man he tied as runner-up, Jack Nicklaus, and the man he lost to, Miller, were two of the most feared competitors in the game. Miller, after speculating that Ballesteros might have won if he'd gone to his 1-iron off the tee instead of stubbornly sticking with his driver, added his voice to the growing chorus of Ballesteros admirers.

Ballesteros had much to savor, but he never lost sight of the crucial fact about the outcome of the Open: He had not won. He was proud of his second place, but he would never again play for second. Three weeks later he won his first international tournament, the Dutch Open, by three strokes. His caddy, David Musgrove, who had seen plenty of tournament golf, was struck by his reaction to the victory. "He did not bat an eyelid. It was as though he were born to win."

Musgrove made this observation to Dudley Doust, Ballesteros's biographer. In *Seve: The Young Champion,* Doust has
recorded a still earlier insight into his subject. Manuel Pinero,
the talented Spanish player who knows Ballesteros as both a
friend and a rival, found Ballesteros sobbing in the locker room
after finishing 12th in the Spanish PGA. Ballesteros was only
seventeen at the time, and as Pinero realized, "He actually
expected to win. He always expects to win."

That first taste of victory at the Dutch Open only whetted
his appetite for more. Two weeks later, he was in Belgium,
playing in an eight-man field for the Swaelens Memorial Trophy, and his opponent was one of his heroes, Gary Player.
Entering the final round, Ballesteros was comfortably ahead of
Player, but he hooked a ball into the trees on the second hole.
Player, from the fairway, pitched dead for a sure birdie, and
Ballesteros, 45 yards from the flag, was facing a swing of two
or possibly three shots. There was a gap in the trees, more a
window than a gap, about head-high and 10 yards from his ball.
Using a 5-iron, Ballesteros punched his ball through that window and watched it pitch short of the green, bounce on, and
run straight into the hole for an eagle.

A week later, playing for the Lancôme Trophy just outside
Paris, Ballesteros made a victim of another of his heroes, Arnold Palmer. At the age of forty-seven, Palmer was past his
prime, but a huge gallery—at the time it was the largest gallery
ever assembled on the Continent for a golf match—turned out
to see him, and Palmer didn't disappoint them. On the front
nine he showed Ballesteros his heels, opening up a four-stroke
lead. Ballesteros didn't crumble. He kept rolling in long putts,
studying Palmer the way a boxer studies his opponent, looking
for a sign of weakness. He saw it at the 15th, when he holed
out for another birdie. "I knew his morale was gone," he told
his biographer, "and that made me feel good." Most golfers
will admit that they hate to lose, but it is a different thing
altogether to relish victory as cold-bloodedly as Ballesteros did.
He seemed to play golf as if there were more at stake than a
check or a trophy. Here the young Ballesteros could be likened

to a matador, who celebrates his triumph by cutting off the ears and tail of his adversary.

Ballesteros was probably no more bent on winning than other great players have been, but his manner was different. He was very young, after all, and he was Spanish. Palmer had always been combative in an earthy, American, all-right-guys-let's-kick-some-butt kind of way, and Nicklaus and Hogan kept their competitive ferocity in check in the time-honored dour, silent, relentless Scottish fashion. Bobby Jones cloaked his will to win in a courtly, playing-fields-of-Eton manner, but he expected everyone, including his opponents, to understand that the objective *was* to win; and no matter how civilized the proceedings on the course might appear, he sometimes felt afterward as if he had fought a "battle with broadswords." Ballesteros, unschooled in any of these niceties, was more tempestuous and predatory. Golf writers casting about for nicknames were soon calling him the Latin Leopard or the Pedrena Panther. There was a savage quality in his approach to the game that prompted Jim Murray, an American journalist, to write, "He goes after a golf course like a lion at a zebra. He doesn't reason with it . . . he tries to hold its head under the water until it stops wriggling." And the drollest of the British writers, Peter Dobereiner, describing Ballesteros's approach to his opponents, especially American opponents, compared him to those Fiji cannibals who devoured Welsh missionaries, believing that they might thereby acquire their virtues.

His competitive edge, in any case, was sharp and gleaming. Along with his classic Latin good looks, he had a classic Latin temperament. ("How many great Latin golfers have there been?" he asks rhetorically. "Only de Vicenzo and Trevino.") He was a dark-haired, dark-eyed kid playing a game that has traditionally been the pastime of cool, blue-eyed Anglos. He might have said of them what John McEnroe, his contemporary, said of his great rival Bjorn Borg, the impassive Swede: "What I do out there on the court is a hundred percent more normal than what he does." Ballesteros didn't throw tantrums, but he rumbled with Vesuvian emotions; he seemed to live or die with every shot he played. To some, his passion for the game was irresistibly fascinating, while to others his confidence came across as unbridled arrogance, his pride as unforgivable hauteur.

His manner didn't sit well with some of the Americans he played against that fall. In the World Match Play Championship in Wentworth, England, his 36-hole match against Hale Irwin—Irwin won, 2 and 1—was marred by a dispute about a rule that allowed the golfers to repair spike marks, but not pitch marks, on the greens. Irwin, thinking that Ballesteros was taking advantage of the rule, made a protest to the officials; and Ballesteros, thinking that his honor had been impugned, was enraged. Then, in December, Ballesteros and Pinero were representing Spain in the World Cup matches when another rules dispute broke out. Pinero had to lift his ball from the fairway, where it had stopped only inches away from Ballesteros's ball. The lift was legal, but Pinero tossed the ball to his caddy, who caught it in a towel—and cleaning was not legal. Jerry Pate, the reigning U.S. Open champion, asked the referee to assess a penalty stroke. The referee didn't know whether the ball had actually been cleaned, and refused. Pate and his partner, Dave Stockton, protested, and before the matter was dropped, the Spaniards had taken offense.

Small incidents, perhaps, but they added up and gave a flavor of vengeance to the Spaniards' victory in the World Cup. When they won—and they won on American soil—Ballesteros burst into tears and embraced Pinero. For the Americans, of course, it was an embarrassing defeat; it was as if a Spanish baseball team had come over and knocked off the Yankees. Golf was one of *our* sports, and the record of wins that Ballesteros kept on piling up didn't make sense in American terms. In 1977 he won seven international titles, three in Europe, two in Japan, one in New Zealand, and one—another World Cup title, this time partnered with Antonio Garrido—at the Wack-Wack Golf Club in the Philippines. When he competed in his first Masters that April, *Golf Digest* splashed him across its cover, over the question, "Can this teen-ager win the Masters?"

The Ballesteros legend was growing steadily. In 1978 he

was all-conquering, winning seven tournaments in seven different countries, including the United States. He had come over to play in the Masters, and entered the Greater Greensboro Open the week before. After two rounds—he shot 72–75—he was 10 strokes behind the leader and had the highest score of those who made the cut. In the third round he shot a 69, the lowest score of the day, and in the final round he ran in putts from everywhere, shot a 66, and won the tournament. He was the only golfer who had ever squeaked past the cut and then overtaken the entire field in the last two days; he was the first foreign nontour member to win an American tournament since 1966 and, altogether, the most remarkable and exciting young golfer to come along in years. Deane Beman offered him membership in the tour, and the PGA offered him an official exemption to compete in the PGA Championship. Ballesteros declined both offers, explaining that he had commitments elsewhere. His biographer reports that he added privately, "Besides, I have already been in the Army, and playing on the American tour is like being in the Army."

That refusal to submit to any authority but his own would become one of his most pronounced traits, as would a reluctance to abandon the European tour. He had become its star, and he crowned his triumphs with his first major championship, the 1979 British Open. In the days before the tournament, Ballesteros played his practice rounds with Roberto de Vicenzo, the durable Argentinian who'd compiled his own impressive list of victories all over the world. De Vicenzo guided him around the Royal Lytham course, famous for its 365 bunkers. All that sand boded well; Ballesteros was a first-class bunker player. He also noted that there were many places outside the fairways where the rough had been trodden down. If he could hit it long—and nobody hit it longer—he could miss the fairways and still leave himself a playable shot to the green. During those practice rounds, Ballesteros blasted away from the tees, looking for safe areas in the rough.

He found them, and kept finding them when the tournament started. In fact, he hit only eight fairways during the first three days of play, but he was at 213—one shot ahead of Nicklaus, and two shots behind Hale Irwin, his playing partner for the last round. It was a chilly, breezy day, and Irwin spent most of it with his head down and his hands in his pockets. He removed one hand at the ninth hole so that he could put a finger to his temple and, figuratively speaking, blow his brains out. Irwin had made the turn in 37, Ballesteros in 34. The Spaniard now had a share of the lead, despite the fact that he had made several excursions into the rough and visited a number of bunkers, including one at the 13th hole, a bunker that happens to be 296 yards from the tee. Ballesteros tried to *carry* it—and failed by only two yards.

He made—he had to make—several exquisite recoveries, but the shot that would be most remembered was his "parking lot" shot, which came at the 16th, a par 4 of 353 yards. The conventional wisdom called for a tee shot down the left of the fairway, but Ballesteros had discovered a landing area in the right rough and sent his tee shot sailing thither. He missed the rough, though not on the fairway side; the ball was found on the other side of the rough, under a car in the parking lot. Ballesteros was not fazed. He knew that he was entitled to relief from the obstacle, and he took it. He paced off the distance to the green, chose a target for his wedge shot on the downhill side of the flag, and dropped the ball in the center of it. The putt was in, and the Open was his.

There were tears on the final green when Ballesteros, embracing one of his brothers, was engulfed by the ecstatic crowd that had cheered him on all week. The British fans had come to look upon him as one of their own. Indeed, Ballesteros had much the same galvanizing effect on European golf that Palmer had had on American golf twenty years earlier: in the most dramatic way, he'd now proven that a European golfer could hold his own against the best Americans. The interloper in this tournament was Irwin, who made sure to congratulate Ballesteros before the crowd broke loose. The Chairman of the Championship Committee had the last word on Ballesteros's victory: "That [he] chose not to use it [the course], but preferred his own, which mainly consisted of hayfields, car parks, grandstands, dropping zones, and even ladies' clothing, was his own affair. Nevertheless, he was a very worthy Open Champion."

The parking lot shot, like the shot at Royal Birkdale, the incredible recovery from the trees at the Swaelens Memorial—these were all storybook shots. Ballesteros had power and finesse, what the Spanish call *manos de plata,* hands of silver. He had all the shots, he had imagination and flair, and now he also had a major title—which meant, among other things, that he was marketable. Soon he was on magazine covers all over Europe and taking on contracts for lucrative endorsements for everything from tomato juice to cars to wristwatches. Though he already had an American agent, Ed Barner, he was courted by that agent *extraordinaire,* Mark McCormack, who handled the business affairs of Arnold Palmer and, for a time, Jack Nicklaus. Ballesteros rebuffed him, preferring as usual to maintain his own sovereignty. He didn't sign on with McCormack, but he did come to a parting of the ways with Barner, setting up his own company, run by two of his brothers, to look after his affairs. The money was pouring in.

There was one more conquest to make, and that would come the next April. The first time he laid eyes on Augusta National, Ballesteros had a familiar feeling. The trees and the lay of the land reminded him of his home course at Pedrena, and he thought to himself, *This is my shade of green.* With its generous fairways and hard, fast greens, the course suited his game perfectly. Each year he had improved on his performance, but for the 1980 Masters he had worked particularly hard. Over the winter he had shortened his backswing, persuaded at last—not by others but by his own experience—to cure his wildness off the tee. He had also spent hours on the hard beaches of Pedrena, putting on the sand, the only available surface that approximated the speed of Augusta's greens. To make sure that he was match-fit, he played in three tournaments in Florida in March, and then he arrived in Augusta a week early to make a thorough reconnaissance of the course.

He was ready. On the first day, wearing a baseball cap—to cut down the glare from the snow-white sand in the bunkers—he used his new, disciplined swing to glide to a 66 and a tie for the lead. The next day he was slashing away at the ball, spraying it everywhere, and still scoring. When he hooked his drive at No. 17 onto the green at No. 7—where his closest competitor, David Graham, happened to be putting—he played his approach shot up the hill and over one of the huge Masters scoreboards, and when the roar told him he was close to pin, he broke into a run to see just how close. Fifteen feet. He birdied the hole, carded a 69, and took a four-stroke lead. When he added a 68 on the third day, he had people talking about the tournament record, 271, shared by Nicklaus and Floyd. He also had people talking about his luck and his cockiness. The blunt Australian golfer, Jack Newton, had heard enough talk in the locker room to prompt him to say, glaring into a television camera, "I've heard some pretty snide, completely uncalled-for remarks from some of your players. America's considered to be tops in professional golf, and here comes a young twenty-three-year-old and he's taken some of the highlight away from your superstars. But the guy's a great player, and the sooner Americans realize it, the better."

Ballesteros didn't break the record, and there were a few sticky moments on the last round when he hit shots at both the 12th and 13th into Rae's Creek, but he held on to win by four strokes, and Fuzzy Zoeller helped him into his first green jacket. He was only four days past his twenty-third birthday, the youngest winner in Masters history, younger by a few months than Jack Nicklaus had been when he first won in 1963.

The next major on the calendar was the U.S. Open, being played at Baltusrol, and Ballesteros arrived as a celebrity, one of golf's certified luminaries. By winning this Open, he could join that elite group of golfers—Jones, Hogan, Snead, Palmer, Nicklaus, Trevino—who have won two majors in a row. The raw Spanish youth had come a very long way in a very short time, and there seemed to be no limit to what he could accomplish.

And then, on the second day of the Open, he missed his tee time. It was a mistake of breathtaking carelessness, and he was disqualified. None of the excuses—the misunderstanding about when he was to tee off, the delay in traffic—justified the mistake or the furious outburst that followed it, culminating in a threat never to play again in the United States. Like his mentor, de Vicenzo, who lost the Masters when he signed an incorrect scorecard, Ballesteros *might* have said, "I am a big stupid"—but he has never been one to find himself at fault. He did calm.down enough to issue a flat, factual statement, but the incident was added to Ballesteros's long list of grievances about the way he was treated in America.

Soon he was having troubles in Europe as well. He had requested appearance money to play in European tournaments, reasoning that if top Americans received such fees, he was entitled to them as well. The European PGA balked, however, and before the storm was over Ballesteros had been thumped by the press and had missed the cut at the 1981 Masters, played shabby golf in all the other majors, forfeited his chance to play on the Ryder Cup team, and withdrawn from the European tour. It seemed as if his fame and fortune had come too quickly, and he was suffering growing pains that, like everything else about him, were large and turbulent.

Let us retrace our steps for a moment. The story of Ballesteros's initiation into golf is a uniquely Spanish version of the caddy's story. Pedrena, the village where he was born—and to which he still returns, like Br'er Rabbit to the brier patch—is the site of one of the most exclusive clubs and finest golf courses in Spain. The young Seve grew up on the outside looking in. From the Ballesteros farm, the second green was an iron shot over a stand of pine trees, and all four boys in the family took to golf like birds to flight. Seve, the youngest by five years, first competed against his older brothers, and he competed as all siblings do, no-holds-barred.

He couldn't keep up with them at first. He had his first golf club by the age of seven, a 3-iron with a whippy stick for a shaft. His brothers were already caddying and playing real golf, but Seve was collecting round pebbles on the beach to use as golf balls and constructing his own courses in the sand or in the dirt around the farm. He was intense, secretive, and already obsessed with the game, or at least with beating his brothers. When he started to caddy and acquired his first club with a steel shaft, another 3-iron, he learned not only to hit full shots with it but to chip and putt, to invent shots out of the rough, even to lay open the face of the club and blast out of traps with it. He and his brothers were the phantoms of the Pedrena golf course, sneaking on when they could, improvising all sorts of games around its edges. Like many another caddy, Ballesteros was playing the game long before he began to think about it, and the key word is *playing.* He wasn't much concerned then with the right way to swing a club, or with following the prescribed route from tee to fairway, and fairway to green. There have been plenty of great musicians who couldn't read a note but simply picked up an instrument and found themselves enthralled by the sounds they were able to elicit from it. Ballesteros's instrument was the 3-iron.

The man who had to run the caddies off the course was the club pro, Ramón Sota. He was also Ballesteros's uncle, and in his day the leading Spanish golfer, winner of several European titles. He had been good enough to win an invitation to the 1965 Masters, where he placed sixth, the highest finish by a Continental player until Seve won in 1980. Sota and his nephew were too often at odds with each other—Sota represented authority—for the young Ballesteros to acquire much in the way of formal instruction, but he was nevertheless improving. At the age of ten, when he played in his first caddy tournament, he shot a 51 for nine holes and finished in tears. At eleven, his score was 42, and he placed second. At twelve, he played a full round and won with a 79. A year later he was playing to a scratch handicap and beginning to beat his brothers. Caddying for one of them in a tournament, he became so incensed with his poor play that he threw down the bag and swore he could do better himself. By the age of sixteen he was living up to his boast; that year he won the Pedrena caddy championship with a 65.

What is remarkable about these beginnings, though, is not only the way they predict the course of Ballesteros's career, both the extraordinary gifts and the temperament of a *primo don,* but also the way they show his isolation from virtually all the traditions and institutions of the game. When he became a card-carrying professional at the age of sixteen, a few scant months after winning his last caddy tournament, he couldn't name golf's four major championships. He had never seen top players in action on a championship course. He had no precedents; no role models except for his brothers, whom he could beat, and his uncle, whom he did not wish to imitate; no idea of what to anticipate on the international tournament circuit; no real conception and certainly no fear of the royal and ancient kingdom that he was about to storm. To return to our musical analogy, the young Ballesteros was in roughly the same position as a boy who decides to become a great virtuoso, having never heard a live performance in a concert hall but only a few scratchy records played on an old phonograph.

One thing more: Ballesteros had by now reached his full height, six feet, and he had the unmistakable grace of a born athlete. His hands were large and his arms were exceptionally long, assets to any golfer. There was only one noticeable physical irregularity, a right shoulder that was lower than the left. Ask Ballesteros how he is able to hit a golf ball so far, and he will stand so that his arms hang loosely at his sides. The right hand is lower than the left. This asymmetry permits him to grip a club and align himself correctly without having to worry about lowering his right shoulder—it is already lowered. That low shoulder may be the result of having carried golf bags for years, but it is also an arguing point for those inclined to believe that he was designed to swing a golf club.

In 1983 Ballesteros won his second Masters. This time he finished each of the first three rounds a stroke behind the leaders and then started the fourth round with a burst that lifted him clear of the field. When he played the first four holes birdie, eagle, par, birdie, there was no catching him. The Masters has a history of exciting finishes, but in both his Masters victories, Ballesteros had turned the tournament into a relatively placid affair. In 1983 this was particularly disappointing, since he was paired with Tom Watson in the last round. The two men were Nicklaus's logical successors, and given the way that the game of golf sooner or later pits the top players against each other, they were sure to meet in a major championship that came down to the wire.

That meeting occurred in the 1984 British Open at St. Andrews. How Watson finished that tournament we have already seen, but Ballesteros's performance was a model of wise restraint. No longer the hotheaded teenager from Spain, he was both more patient and more subdued on the course. In fact, a year earlier he had been criticized for his caution in the U.S. Open at Oakmont, where he persisted in using his 1-iron off the tee even though the fairways had been drenched by heavy rains. Drives were sitting right where they landed; there was no danger of a ball running into the rough, and Ballesteros was giving up 50 yards on every driving hole.

This more conservative strategy was working at St. Andrews. Ballesteros stayed close to the lead, and in the last round, playing just ahead of Watson, the Spaniard came to the 17th in a dead heat for the lead. The 17th, the Road Hole, is a 461-yard par 4, but Ballesteros had yet to par it during the tournament. This time he did. He then smashed a big drive at No. 18 and pitched close to the flag. The putt was in for a birdie. On the two closing holes, it was Ballesteros who applied the pressure. Though decidedly more prudent, he was still one of the toughest finishers in the game, a golfer who could produce the key shots when he had to. He was one of the few golfers who was never accused of choking.

His scorecard for that last round would have been held up for emulation by the Scots. Instead of setting par figures for each hole, they used to speak of playing a round in "level 4s," and that is almost precisely what Ballesteros had done. Consider his numbers:

444 444 424 – 34
444 444 443 – 35 — 69

There was nothing mercurial about that card, and it spoke volumes about the change in Ballesteros. Though still plagued by occasional wildness off the tee, he was more firmly in control of his game than he had ever been. It was as if the blaze and crackle of those first years had been simply the high combustion of a fire starting up on a bed of kindling; now the fire was no less hot but a good deal steadier. Ballesteros did not sound like a raw youth but like a man who could appreciate the full weight of what he had just accomplished: "I feel great to beat the best man in the world, and at the home of golf, St. Andrews." He added, with wonder and a touch of humility, what golfers have been saying for centuries: "This game is very great and very strange."

Ballesteros had reached the pinnacle of golf. He didn't win a major championship in 1985, though he was in pursuit at the Masters. He tied for fifth at the U.S. Open, one of his best showings in that event; he has not fared especially well at either the U.S. Open or the PGA, where the fairways are narrowed and the rough more punishing than at Augusta. Ballesteros is very much aware that his poor showings in those two tournaments are marks against him, for he has come to judge himself as Nicklaus and Watson judge themselves, on the basis of his record in the majors. He summed up his 1985 season by saying, "I won six tournaments but no majors. That is like when you go fishing and catch trout, but no salmon."

Now, back at Augusta, the place in the United States where he felt most at home, he had another salmon on the line. He hadn't landed it yet, but the hook was set.

The juncture of the two par 3s, the 6th and the 16th, is one of the great gathering places at Augusta National.

*Photo © Brian Morgan*

After running in a 25-foot eagle putt at No. 15 on the second day of play, the emotional Ballesteros roared triumphantly, knowing he had just taken command of the tournament.

*Photo © Brian Morgan*

The defending champion, West German Bernhard Langer, scrutinized his putts with microscopic attention. The slippery bent-grass greens are the pride, and terror, of Augusta National.

*Photo © Brian Morgan*

In his long career Nicklaus had never travelled at such a scorching pace over the closing holes of a tournament, nor had he played with more visible emotion. Father and son embraced each other as they left the final green.

*Photo © Leonard Kamsler*

Jackie had challenged his father to make an eagle at No. 15—and when Nicklaus Senior did, the crowd sent up what may have been the loudest cheer in the history of golf.

Jackie was at his father's shoulder throughout the tournament. After conferring on this long birdie putt on the shadow-streaked 10th green, Nicklaus Senior knocked it in.

*Photo © Leonard Kamsler*

Even though Tom Watson had his chances on the last day of the tournament, the putts he needed just wouldn't fall.

*Photo © Brian Morgan*

After a brilliant shot to the 13th green in the final round, Ballesteros and his brother, Vicente, looked jubilant as they marched toward the green. An eagle here gave Ballesteros what looked like an ironclad lead.

*Photo © Brian Morgan*

A birdie at No. 15 in the second round helped Greg Norman climb out of the hole he had dug with a four-putt double bogey at No. 10.

*Photo © Brian Morgan*

One of the few putts Price missed all day was at the 18th. After the ball curled out of the cup, he said, "It's as if the hand of Bobby Jones had flicked it away. Sixty-three is enough!"

*Photo © Leonard Kamsler*

After a string of four birdies, Norman wanted to win the tournament with a fifth. But his approach to the 18th flew deep into the gallery. "I let my ego get the best of me," he said.

*Photo © Brian Morgan*

Tom Kite needed this birdie putt at the 18th to tie Nicklaus—and couldn't believe it when the ball tailed off at the cup.

*Photo © Leonard Kamsler*

Nicklaus, with the help of Bernhard Langer, dons his sixth green jacket.

# 6

# A New Record

April in Georgia is a fickle thing, and when play began on Saturday morning, it seemed as if the season had advanced overnight from early spring to high summer. The southwest wind had finally puffed itself out, and the air was still and heavy. It was far more humid than it had been during the first two days of the tournament, and the greens, which had been watered overnight, were unmistakably slower. In addition, the greens committee seemed to have relented, and most of the pins had been placed in somewhat more forgiving positions. It took no time at all for the players to discover that not only could they fire their approach shots right at the flags, but they could also stroke their putts more firmly. For the first two days Augusta National had played like a lion, but today the course was meek as a lamb.

The stage was set, then, for what the pros call "moving day," since the third round so often brings major fluctuations to the leader board. The cut has been made—in this Masters the cut eliminated forty-four players, exactly half of the field—and there is every incentive, especially for the players well off the pace, to go all out. They have nothing to lose. A bold round can get them back into the hunt or at least earn them a place in the top twenty-four and an invitation to next year's Masters.

When Nick Price teed off just before noon, he was too far

in back of the leaders to set his sights any higher than the top twenty-four. With rounds of 79 and 69, he'd made the cut with a stroke to spare, but he was nine shots behind Ballesteros. And even though that 69 had salved his pride, he was still smarting from the embarrassment of the first round, which included six three-putts. He had been unnerved by the speed and slope of these bent-grass greens, and he was too disgusted when he came off the course on Thursday to think of practicing. The next morning, though, he spent extra time on the putting green. What he worked on was not his putting stroke—that was sound enough—but his head. Price likes to play rapidly, and he belongs to the "miss it quick" school of thought. He has a tendency to hurry when things start to go wrong. On the practice green he made himself slow down and cultivate a patient, almost Zen-like attitude. "I said to myself, *look* at what you've got to putt. *Look* at the surface. *Look* at all the breaks and contours. *Look* at everything and take it all in. Instead of just putting another twenty-footer, *look* at the line. I tried almost to feel that I *was* the ball, and straight-away that effort to concentrate made a difference."

His putting on Friday still wasn't anything to get excited about, but it wasn't his undoing, either. He sank the short ones and kept the long ones close. His ball-striking was crisp, as it had been throughout the spring, and his 69 gave his confidence a boost; it was the first time he'd broken par at Augusta National. He was playing in his second Masters—he missed the cut in 1984—and his best previous round had been a 76.

Price, who grew up in Rhodesia, or what is now Zimbabwe, was listed on the pairing sheets as a South African—but the Masters officials aren't the only ones who have a hard time placing him. He lives in Florida and carries a British passport; and like Ballesteros, he has campaigned on several different continents. Yet it is easier to account for his travels than to know where to place him in golf's hierarchy. He is probably best known as the runner-up in the 1982 British Open at Royal Troon, or as the winner of the 1983 World Series of Golf, his only victory on the American tour; he looked invincible as he cruised to a wire-to-wire victory. The next year he was running away with the Canadian Open until he faded in the last round. His best performance in 1985 came at the PGA, where he fought his way into contention with a third round 65. With that sort of record in important tournaments, you might have expected to find him in contention on a weekly basis, but often enough he was struggling to make the cut. In short, Price had a reputation for blowing hot and cold, but he was most likely to warm up in a big event.

He got off to a wobbly start when he poked his opening drive into the fairway bunker that guards the turn of the dogleg. The big hitters can fly that bunker, but Price's game depends more on control than on length. Besides, he is a right-to-left player, and this first hole is a dogleg right. Price cordially despises this particular tee shot, but the shot that galled him most on the first hole was his putt to save par. All he could do was splash the ball out of the bunker, but he pitched nicely onto the green—and babied the putt. Bogey.

As he walked to the second tee, Price did some thinking out loud with his caddy, Irishman David McNeilly. "If we're going to do any good," he said, "I'm going to have to get more aggressive with my putting." That kind of resolution, as every golfer knows, more often than not belongs in the category of wishful thinking, and Price's next putt was one to make him gag on his words. He'd wedged his third shot on the long par 5 to within six feet of the cup, but those six feet were downhill and delicate. He was facing a runaway putt with a big twist in it, the hardest kind of putt to play boldly. Price stroked it into the middle of the cup.

It was the most heartening putt he'd made all week. Over on the edge of the green, McNeilly went into his birdie dance, a gleeful Irish jig that he would perform again at the fifth, the sixth, and the eighth, for Price was suddenly white-hot. He was driving the ball with authority and knocking down the flags with his irons. His 5-iron at the fifth was only 12 feet from the hole, and his 6-iron at the sixth was 15 feet away. His birdie at the eighth came when he wedged to 6 feet. His wedge had been especially deadly all week; on the practice tee, he'd been lobbing balls at a pin 70 yards out and rattling it time after time. The wedge was his club for the tournament, the club that set his rhythm and dictated his strategy on the par 5s—why try to get home in two when you can wedge it within spitting distance of the hole?

Price made the turn in 33. He stung his drive on the 10th and hit a 6-iron that shaved the pin and left him a 4-footer, another grisly little twister that he drained. Entering Amen Corner, he stood at four under. All the elements of his game were meshing like clockwork, but he was leery of the pond that guards the left front of the 11th green. Instead of flirting with it, he aimed his 5-iron approach some 15 feet to the right of the flag. The ball was dead on line and finished pin-high. The putt fell. Price reached the 12th with an 8-iron and dispatched a 20-footer, this one with two twists in it. He was reading Augusta's cryptic greens as easily as you or I might read the big numbers on the scoreboard. He laid up on the 13th, played another precision wedge, made his fourth birdie in a row. He was now seven under par, and he had a question for McNeilly.

"Do you know what the record on this course is?"

"No," said the Irishman.

"It's sixty-four."

"Let's go for it."

"Don't worry," Price said. "I'm not backing off."

For Price there was more at stake than the course record. As he strung his birdies together, he was well aware that he was lifting himself right back into contention in the tournament. He'd already overtaken most of the field, speeding past them like a fire engine through stalled traffic, and he was closing in fast on the leaders. He'd raced from four over par to three under, and suddenly there were only three men ahead of him, and not all that far ahead, either. Price was playing the round of his life, and he had forgotten all about the invitation for next year. He had resurrected his chances to win *this* Masters.

This was a different kind of pressure, a pressure Price had felt most keenly at Royal Troon. He had played solid golf during the first three days of the tournament, and he entered the fourth round one stroke in back of Bobby Clampett, who had set a fast pace from the start, at one point leading by as many as seven strokes. Then Clampett went to pieces and gave what is still regarded, in the annals of collapse, as a classic perform- ance. He has been a different golfer ever since.

Price inherited the lead.

He was ahead by two strokes with six holes to play, and he held on until the 15th, where he hooked his drive. He had a clean enough lie in the rough, but there was a little ridge in front of him. Though he needed a 2-iron to reach the green, he knew he couldn't get the ball up over the ridge unless he used a more lofted club. He chose a 4-iron, and nailed it—but the ball caught the top of the ridge, kicked way off line, and ended up in a trap that wasn't even close to the green. A bad drive, a mental error, and before he quite understood what had happened, Price had double bogeyed the hole. He was shaken. His lead had slipped away. He dropped another shot on the way in, and presented the victory to a disbelieving Tom Watson, who had finished his own round long before.

Price has thought long and hard about his loss at the Brit- ish Open, and he doesn't mince words when he describes those last few holes. "I was dazed, stunned, bewildered," he admits, displaying a candor that is rare among professional golfers. At the same time, he was determined to extract whatever wisdom he could from the experience. There were two important les- sons. The first was that he had the potential to win a major championship. The second was that if he wanted to fulfill that potential, he was going to have to develop a game that would hold up under pressure.

Earlier that same year he had begun to rebuild his swing. He was essentially a "natural" player (I put the word in quota- tion marks, remembering that Hogan once growled, "There is nothing natural about the golf swing"). Price had picked up the rudiments of the game as most kids do, catch-as-catch-can. An exceptional athlete and a talented mimic, he fashioned a swing that showed the influence of the four golfers he most ad- mired—Palmer, Player, Nicklaus, and his older brother, Tim. That hybrid swing worked, though, and at the age of seventeen, Price made his first trip to the United States to enter the Junior World Tournament in California. He won, and the next year he played as an amateur on both the South African and European tours.

After a tour of duty in the Rhodesian Air Force, he was ready to turn professional. In 1980 he won the South African Masters and the Swiss Open, placed second in four other events, and seemed to be on the verge of putting it all together. The next year he was mired in a slump, discouraged by the weather in Europe—"I was getting tired of playing in three sweaters and rain gear every day"—and convinced that if he wanted to compete at the highest level, he needed a better understanding of the golf swing.

He traveled to Florida to work with Dave Leadbetter, a fellow Zimbabwean who coaches a number of touring pros. He hit thousands of balls and analyzed hundreds of swings on videotape. He quickly began to master the principles of a correct and efficient swing—a professional swing, free of clutter and unfunctional decor—and, also, to realize just how deeply his own bad habits were ingrained. Leadbetter pointed out, for instance, that instead of cocking his wrists fully at the top of the backswing, he tended to cock them on the way down. It is one of many habits that, years later, Price would still be struggling to overcome. "You can't just change overnight," Price says, "not if you want to go out and perform. You have to be patient and nibble away at your faults."

The last and most critical stage of his education as a golfer had begun. That summer at Troon he realized how tantalizingly close he was to the top. Only one stroke had separated him from Watson, one stroke and that extra, elusive quality that always separates championship golfers from all the rest. Watson calls it "heart," and Bobby Jones once called it "the sheer delicatessen." Price calls it "character," and—here was the third lesson of Troon—he realized that no one could teach it to him. He would have to find it within himself.

So when he got on a roll at Augusta, Nick Price had something to prove to himself. His golf had been airtight all day long, but as he came into the homestretch, to play the last holes in front of a gallery that by now knew he was taking the course apart and challenging for the lead, he was going to have to depend on more than a hot hand. He was going to need that extra something.

At the 14th, he missed his putt—and his fifth birdie in a row—by an eyelash. He resisted temptation at the par-5 15th and played the hole as he had planned, laying up short of the pond and then producing a pretty wedge that plumped down four feet from the flag. A thunderous ovation greeted him as he made his way to the green, passing in front of the jam-packed grandstand. "When I crossed that bridge, Sarazen's Bridge, the people started clapping and cheering. They wanted to be there on that particular day, at that particular Masters, when the record was broken. They wanted to witness it, and I wanted to do it. Jack Nicklaus and Arnold Palmer must have experienced that kind of emotion from a gallery hundreds of times, but I've only felt it once. It's a great feeling. You have no idea what it does for your ego, if you want to call it that, or for your confidence."

This four-footer would tie him for the record, but he didn't waste any time over it. He started it out three inches left of the hole and let it break right into the heart of the cup. When it fell, McNeilly almost jumped out of his caddy smock and Price took one long gliding sidestep and raised his putter aloft. That putt had cinched it. He still had three holes, three tough holes, to play, but there was no doubt in his mind that he could keep pouring it on.

The pin at No. 16 was cut on the low side of the green, the side near the water. Price didn't take aim at the flag. Instead, he played his tee shot onto the high side of the green, expecting it to check up and roll back down toward the cup. Like every other iron shot he'd hit, this was struck exactly as he wanted, but for a moment he thought he'd overdone it. The ball released slightly and looked as if it might perch on the little plateau at the back of the green. Just when it seemed to have died, though, it turned over, and then it trickled down the slope. The ball came to rest about three feet short of the cup. Price sank the putt, and crossed a frontier. No one had ever stood at nine under par at Augusta National.

All he had to do now was par the last two holes, but he was in no mood to ease up. "All I was thinking then was birdie— one shot on the fairway, one shot on the green, one putt in the hole, and that's it." His putt on the 17th looked in all the way but didn't quite have the speed. Par. One more hole to play.

The last hole, like the first hole, requires a fade off the tee, and Price didn't produce it. He hooked his drive into the left rough, and with the flag 190 yards away on the upper tier of the green, and a bunker directly in his line of flight, he was confronted with his most difficult approach shot of the day. He hit a 4-iron, and he couldn't have hit it any better. It rolled to the top of the green, leaving him 30 feet from the cup. Price was determined, after that putt at No. 17, not to leave this one short. The ball streaked toward the cup—Price thought it was in, but McNeilly, horrified, was sure it was 5 feet too strong— careened around the rim like a tiny white bobsled, and curled out. Price would say later, "It was as if the hand of Bobby Jones reached up and flicked it away. Sixty-three is enough!"

Enough, indeed. Half a century before, in 1936, Bobby Jones completed a practice round in 64 strokes. It was appropriate that Jones, having retired from competitive golf, should have established a quiet precedent, leaving to others the honor of setting the official record. In 1940 Lloyd Mangrum shot an opening-round 64, a mark that wasn't equaled until 1965, when Jack Nicklaus virtually rewrote the Masters record book. In those days he was the longest hitter in the game, and he simply overpowered the course. His 72-hole total that year was 271, and his winning margin was nine strokes; both figures are records that still stand. Since 1965 four players—Hale Irwin, Miller Barber, Maurice Bembridge, and Gary Player—have tied the single-round record.

Price had bettered all of them. There may be no such thing as perfection in golf, but he had played a nearly flawless round. He had missed only two fairways, and he hit every green in regulation except for No. 1 and No. 3, a green which is not only shaped like a football but contoured like one. It takes real legerdemain to get a ball to balance on its rounded surface, and Price's wedge shot rolled just off the back edge and into the fringe. His ten birdies set another Masters record, and his 63 brought the single-round record into line with the record at the other major championships.

Inevitably, there were those who saw the round as a fluke and pointed out that the playing conditions were the easiest in the history of the Masters. The field averaged just under 71, four strokes lower than on Thursday, and a full stroke lower than the next-best scoring day on record.

It goes without saying that scoring records are made under favorable conditions—Johnny Miller's U.S. Open record was set on a rain-softened Oakmont—and Price's 63 was a full four strokes better than anybody else was able to shoot that Saturday. What's more, he had finished the day with a red 5 beside his name on the scoreboard, giving the leaders a number to shoot at. Only one of them, as it turned out, would bring in a lower three-day total. Most important of all, as far as Nick Price was concerned, he had passed a private test with flying colors. Maybe he was playing over his head—anybody who shoots a 63 at Augusta National is playing over his head—but, in golf, one definition of character is the ability to play over your head when it counts most.

# 7

# Saturday

Saturday is "moving day," but nobody moved as far or as fast as Nick Price. Over the course of the hazy afternoon, one player after another would make a dash toward the top, only to subside again. There were three 67s, seven 68s, and seven 69s—a total of eighteen rounds (including Price) under 70, as opposed to four on Thursday and six on Friday—but when the last putts had been holed out and the numbers duly recorded, only a few names on the leader boards had changed.

T. C. Chen had faded to a 75, and Danny Edwards's slot on the board had been given to Price. Edwards had played the course in even par, losing ground to over half the field, but the golfer who felt the most galling disappointment had to be Bill Kratzert. While others were making birdies in bunches, he began his round with two pars and a rash of bogeys, three in succession. He never recovered. To his credit, he kept playing full-blooded golf shots, like his long approach at No. 10, where he just missed his birdie, and his even longer and bolder approach at No. 15. The pin was cut near the front of the green, dangerously close to the pond, and most players made sure they carried the water with plenty to spare. Kratzert cut it fine. From 225 yards out, he laced a 3-iron that cleared the bank by inches and finished less than 10 feet from the hole. He missed the eagle putt. He might as well have been putting with a sledgehammer. Some days you have the touch, and some days you don't—but what a hard day not to have it! Kratzert's dream of winning the Masters was receding hole by hole, and by the time he had completed his round, with a 76, it was dust.

Ben Crenshaw was having his tribulations as well. At two under when he teed off, he quickly went to four under with birdies at No. 2 and No. 5, and there were only two men ahead of him, Ballesteros and Price. It seemed just possible that he really had regained his old form and that his game had jelled at just the right time. When he made the turn, he was counseling himself—as he had in 1984, when he won the tournament—to set up well, to hit the ball with good timing, to put it on the fairways and the greens. The short game would take care of itself. With his soft touch, and with his veteran caddy, Carl Jackson, to help him read the greens, he could stay in until the end of the tournament if he could just keep the ball in play.

He was in the fringe at No. 10, the hole where, two years before, he rolled in a swinging 60-foot birdie putt—a putt that broke 8 feet—to pin down the lead for good. Now he had a chip of about the same distance, and he botched it. The ball streaked 20 feet past the hole. Crenshaw does not often betray anger on the course, but he stamped his foot, hard, and pretended to break his club over his knee, not just in fun. The putt coming back was downhill, and Crenshaw missed it. For the remainder of the day, he would fight to get the ball in the hole, finishing with a 40 on the back nine. "The short game, the touch, is the slowest part of the game to come back, and it just wasn't there when I needed it," Crenshaw said, but the explanation was cold comfort. His opportunity to celebrate his recovery with another victory at Augusta had slipped away.

While Crenshaw's fortunes were declining, Tom Kite's were on the rise. Their careers have been linked for years. They both grew up in Texas and had the same teacher, Harvey Penick, who is certainly flexible in his teaching methods. The two men were as different as a hare and a tortoise, but Penick made winners of them both. Crenshaw, of course, was the hare, blessed with an abundance of talent and instinct, while Kite had the humbler gifts of the tortoise, patience and perseverance. The two went to the same college, the University of

Texas, and shared the NCAA championship in 1972. Even then Crenshaw overshadowed his teammate, winning the NCAA honors by himself in 1971 and 1973, and his arrival on the tour was heralded with trumpets. With his Hollywood good looks, his innate gentlemanly courtesy, his affection for the game, and his knowledge of its lore, Crenshaw quickly became one of the most popular of the professionals. In interviews he spoke straight from the heart—"I love this course Bobby Jones designed, and I love this tournament that he and Mr. Roberts started," he said after winning the Masters—and his sincerity came through. On the course he played a wide-open game and usually seemed to be following his own yellow brick road, one that led him—and his galleries—wide-eyed and wondering through all sorts of fabulous perils.

Kite, by contrast, was a more methodical player who preferred the straight and narrow, proceeding deliberately and with all due caution from Point A to Point B. Despite his walk, a splay-footed ramble that looks nonchalant, he was one of the most analytical players in golf, and you could almost see him plotting his shots in geometric, blueprint lines. Consistency was his strong suit, and consistency, as Kite understood, could sometimes be "a dirty word." While his fellow professionals could and did appreciate the excellence of his play week in and week out, year in and year out, the galleries don't always warm up to a golfer who makes a round look too easy or too clinical. Lacking Crenshaw's flair, and his knack for communicating to the public—Kite tends to be guarded when he talks to the media, confining himself to comments about the details of the game—he quietly went about forging one of the most impressive records on the tour.

Kite won the Rookie of the Year Award in 1973 and steadily improved on that initial performance. His best year came in 1981, when he replaced Tom Watson as the leading money winner. Though he had only one tournament victory that year, he finished in the top ten in twenty-one of the twenty-six tournaments he entered, an astounding percentage. Kite likes to measure his performance by his top ten finishes, believing that if he's stayed that close to the lead throughout a tournament, he has played well enough to win. "I can control what I do out there," he says, "but I have no control over what anyone else does." In 1981, and again in 1982, Kite won the Vardon Trophy, an award given to the player with the lowest stroke average on the tour. He is one of the only golfers who can look back on a lengthy career that is not marred by a slump—though if you mention that word to Kite, he grins and tries not to correct you. By his own exacting standards, he has been in and out of many a slump.

Still, if you graphed Kite's career, you would have one rising line and then a high plateau. Crenshaw's line looks more like the Dow-Jones with the jitters, and yet in terms of victories—Kite had won eight tournaments, Crenshaw ten—and in terms of disappointments in major championships, they continued to have much in common. Both had established the credentials to win a major and failed to do so; they were becoming rivals for the depressing honor of being the best player never to have won a major. They had both come close in the 1978 British Open at St. Andrew's and tied for the runner-up position, behind Nicklaus. When Crenshaw broke through and won the Masters in 1984, one of his victims was Tom Kite, who had been leading the tournament by a stroke at the end of the third round. Kite does not have to be reminded that he dumped a 7-iron into Rae's Creek at the 12th, took a triple bogey, and played the final round in 75.

Kite's best finish in the U.S. Open was an eighth at Winged Foot in 1974, and he tied for fourth in the 1981 PGA, but he had challenged most consistently for a major title right here at Augusta. Since his first Masters as a professional in 1975, Kite had done everything but win. In those eleven tournaments, he had missed the cut only once, in 1985. The other ten times he finished with a four-round total that was under par, and he was out of the top ten only once. His stroke average at Augusta National, 71.7, was the lowest of any player who had not won the tournament, and the fourth lowest among all players. The three men with a better average were Jack Nicklaus, Tom Watson, and Seve Ballesteros.

While Kite was proud of his Masters record, he knew that

a good many followers of the game had consigned him to the rank of super journeyman, one of those golfers who was simply not destined to catch hold of the brass ring. Kite tried to put both his reputation and his past performances out of mind. When he arrived in Augusta, he tried to settle down to business—and insofar as it was possible, to business as usual. His approach on the course is to play every shot as if he were on the practice range, and he tries to approach each tournament, including the Masters, as if it were any other tournament. "I know the Masters isn't just any other tournament," Kite concedes, but he does everything he can not to put any extra pressure on himself. He was determined to stick to all his normal routines.

So far he had done so, despite a second round of 74. Kite does not like playing in the wind, which introduces too many variables and deprives a golfer of control. This calm Saturday was much more to his liking, and he played the outward nine in 34—seven pars, two birdies. He added three more pars when he made the turn. His routine calls for him to walk to his ball, check the lie, remove the course yardage book from his back hip pocket, pace off the distance to the nearest sprinkler head, and then discuss with Mike Carrick, who has been his caddy for years, anything that needs discussing—the pin placement, the contours of the green, the potential risks of the shot he is contemplating. When he is satisfied that he has taken everything into account, and only when he is satisfied, he selects his club. Still positioned behind the ball, he takes a long, lingering look at his target. He then steps up, takes his stance, aligned toward his target but with his clubhead a foot or so from the ball, and takes an easy practice swing, just to get a feel for the clubhead, and for tempo. He has decided on the shot he wants to make, and the only thing he tells himself as he sets up is "Take the club back slow." He settles his weight on his spikes, and he looks three times—not twice, not four times—at his target. He waggles his club in a short, low arc. The routine is so calibrated that you could set your watch by it, and it gets results.

Kite wasn't in any real trouble on this round until No. 13,

where he hit his second shot into Rae's Creek. The creek is only a few yards wide and a few inches deep where it curls around the front of the green, and the ball was only half-submerged. Kite waded in—no routine on this shot—and splashed it out to within a club length of the hole. He missed the birdie putt, but he'd been looking at a bogey and came away with a par that seemed to spur him on. The next four holes he put on his own show, featuring astute course management and accurate iron play. At No. 14 he made sure that he was well over the crest at the front of the green but left his birdie putt a fraction short. He birdied No. 15 when, again taking the safe route, he was at the back of the widest part of the green in two. The pin on No. 16 was close to the water, and Kite played the hole as Nick Price had, bringing his tee shot into the right of the green and letting it run down toward the hole. Another birdie. At No. 17 the only route to the flag was straight over a bunker, and Kite took it; here he had reason to be grateful for his big drive—at five feet eight and 155 pounds, he is not among the long hitters on the tour, but this week he had been driving exceptionally well—since it left him with only a pitching wedge to this 400-yard par 4. The ball sat down a foot from the hole. Kite had reeled off three birdies in a row and played himself into a tie for second place, trailing only Ballesteros. He was looking at a 67 until he foozled a tiny putt for par at the finishing hole and registered his only bogey of the day.

That bogey meant that he finished in a dead heat with his playing partner, Tom Watson. They had identical three-day scores: 70–74–68—212. If Watson had scrambled on his first round and mishit a few key shots on his second round, yet a third Watson had played the course today. He hit the ball cleanly from the first hole to the last, but he seemed baffled by the greens. At the 14th he three-putted for his only bogey of the day, but he missed a makable eagle putt at No. 15 and rimmed out his eight-foot birdie putt at No. 17. On a day when he seemed to have lasers in his irons, he was hardly overjoyed with a 68. "Except for one bad club selection," he said at the end of the day, still thinking about that shot in the creek at No.

12, "I'd be leading the tournament." And when he ran his eye over the leader board, he added, "I hope an American wins. And I hope his initials are T. W."

Watson and Kite had closed the gap on Ballesteros, but they were playing in front of Norman, Langer, and Nakajima. All three of them had kept pace. After a slow start—perhaps to adjust to the ideal scoring conditions—Nakajima had rallied with four birdies on the back nine to get home with his third consecutive subpar round, a 71. Langer spread his birdies out among the par 5s—he birdied No. 2, No. 8, and No. 15—and managed to avoid a bogey, though he made the round interesting by charging his approach putts. He was certainly giving his putts every chance, but he was consistently three or four feet past the hole, leaving himself those come-backers that are about as long as a snake, and about as mean. On the greens he studied these putts from every conceivable angle, from both sides and both ends; he used the plumb-bob method and his own "blinders" method, putting his hands up like the blinders on a horse; he got down low to squint along the line at grass level; in short, he did everything but set up a tripod and conduct a survey of the green. All this sighting took time, and it didn't seem to be contributing to Langer's peace of mind. Not too many years ago he had a well-known case of the "yips," that dread disease that afflicts the anxious putter; and the way he was laboring on the greens, it looked as if it could recur.

Greg Norman had gotten himself back into the tournament with a round that was pure Norman. He played the front nine in even par, holding steady at two under for the tournament and fast running out of holes. His back was against the wall, and that is where he seems to like it. He gave himself "a good talking to"—I'm only guessing, but I imagine it was pretty savage—and birdied his way through Amen Corner. Then, like Kite, he turned the 17th into a drive-and-pitch hole, making his birdie from eight feet. He was right back in it.

Even though he had scored so much better on the back nine, Norman hadn't overpowered the course. Despite his reputation as a serve-and-volley golfer, he has worked hard to improve his accuracy with his pitching clubs and his short game. At No. 12, he cut an 8-iron that flew high above the pines—nobody hits the ball higher than Norman, and he had to tilt his head back to follow its flight, like a man looking up an elevator shaft—and set up his birdie. With his length off the tee, he seemed to have another sure birdie at No. 13; he was playing a 6-iron to the green. He went for the pin, cut at the left of the green, and pulled the shot just enough so that it hit the bank and kicked way down the grassy slope. Now he had to get back up the bank, and he had no green to work with. What to do? Norman went to his putter. He rolled the ball up the hill and through the fringe 30 yards away, letting it pop out onto the putting surface. It was a terrific improvisation, and he made the putt. At the next hole, he hit a 9-iron a little fat and left it exactly where no one wants to be, at the front of a green with a huge crest between him and the hole. This particular green looks as if it might be the work of a sculptor whose medium is bent grass, and the piece could be entitled "Wave Breaking at Waikiki." Using a wedge, Norman pitched the ball so that it caught the wave and rode it like a surfer, expiring a foot from the hole.

In short, Norman showed that his game had more than a single dimension. He'd always had power to burn, but his back nine was an exhibition of finesse. Having taken up golf at the relatively advanced age of seventeen, he believed that he was finally catching up with players like Ballesteros, for instance, who had a ten-year head start on him. In fact, Norman has often thanked Ballesteros for helping him with his short game when the two were campaigning together in Europe.

Ballesteros was still on the course when Norman completed his round, and it looked as if they might be paired together in the last twosome of the final round. With a total of 210, Norman was the leader "in the clubhouse," which means that he had the lowest score of any of the golfers who had completed their round, but he wasn't in the clubhouse. Instead, he was obligingly answering questions for the television crew, and he emphasized, as he had all week, the crucial importance of using your judgment. "The golf course was benign today, but when the heat's on, the leaders aren't shooting a lot of birdies. You've got to respect the old girl," he said, and Augusta National was the *old girl.* "When the heat's on, you've still got to be careful."

Several Ballesteros watchers thought that he might be playing a bit too carefully. As he had yesterday, he was leaving the ball below the hole, but usually too far below to give himself a real chance for a birdie. On the front side, his only birdie came at the third, a short par 4, when he stopped his pitch four feet from the cup. He then ran off eleven straight pars, and you had to wonder whether he had decided to attack only on the par 5s (he couldn't attack No. 13, since he pushed his tee shot to the right, as he had on Friday; this time he heeded his discretion and laid up short of the creek). When I asked Ballesteros if his strategy had changed for the third round, Ballesteros replied that he hadn't felt especially sharp. He sounded like Norman, with a Spanish twist, when he added, "I really respect this golf course. I don't come to the first tee and say, I am going to eat this place up. No, I approach the course with respect, and just go easy and wait till the score comes. At Augusta, if you lose patience, the golf course will bite you very quick."

Whatever the explanation, Ballesteros looked flat. By the time he reached No. 15, he knew that the field was gaining on him, and he roused himself, drilling a 4-iron to the green and two-putting for his birdie. He almost made it two in a row when his tee shot at No. 16 finished only eight feet from the hole. He wanted this putt in the worst way, but left it a trifle on the high side. Muttering, he retired to the edge of the green and gave himself a brief, agitated putting clinic.

At this point he was seven under par, a stroke ahead of Norman, and he opened up another birdie possibility with a blast off the tee at No. 17. He followed that with a loose pitch and a feeble lag putt that finished 12 feet short of the hole. When he missed the par-saver, he dropped back into a tie for the lead he had managed to hold all day long. A few minutes later, when his wayward approach to No. 18 found a bunker, he lost the lead altogether and opened the door to a Sunday free-for-all.

Ballesteros's weak finish—he'd just frittered away a pair of precious strokes—took everyone by surprise. Nevertheless, the Spaniard professed to like his position. He had this to say about the difference between playing with the lead and coming from behind: "At Augusta, it is much easier to win from behind. That is true at any tournament. In golf you are looking for the first spot. If you are in the lead, you are already there. There's nothing out there in front of you. So, mentally, it makes you play conservative. You are already in the lead, and you are afraid to lose. Coming from behind, you are not afraid. There is nothing to lose. It is all to win."

Several young Americans had to like their chances better after Ballesteros had faltered so unexpectedly. The group at 214 included Tway, Koch, Pavin, and McCumber, all of whom had shot 71s. McCumber had started out like a house afire, with an eagle at No. 2 and a birdie at No. 4, but then he had cooled off. The lowest he'd been able to get was four under. For one brief, glorious moment Pavin got to three under; he cut a 4-wood that settled down on the 15th green as softly as the proverbial butterfly with sore feet, and he sank a 2-footer for an eagle. At No. 16, Pavin, who plays a fade, had to fly his ball over the lake toward a flag cut not more than 20 feet from the water. Pavin missed his landing area by 10 feet, but his margin for error on this particular shot was only 5 feet. The ball kicked off the bank and into the water. He double bogeyed that hole, and made birdie on No. 17 to finish off an unusual three-hole parlay: eagle, double bogey, birdie. You don't see that every day.

A young player who'd gotten himself into contention and stayed there was Donnie Hammond, known to his fans as Hambone. Slight and lanky, with a dip in his knee on his backswing—he looks as if he is genuflecting when he takes the club back—he knew he was on the way to a good round when his approach at the second hole hit the flagstick. He put together a round of 32–35—67, heady stuff for a golfer whose only previous visit to Augusta had been eleven years earlier when he worked as a gallery guard. He was wired when, leaving the course, he was whisked away to the television cameras in Butler Cabin. "It was great just to know where that room was," he said. When Musburger asked him how he felt about the possibility of being paired with Ballesteros, Hammond blurted out, "I might just show Seve a thing or two."

One older American golfer, Jack Nicklaus, had also moved into position at 214. Like so many others, he had made nearly all his headway in one rush when he birdied the 8th and 9th, parred the 10th, and added two more birdies at the 11th and 12th. His run ended when his second shot at No. 13, a 2-iron, landed on the far bank of the creek but rolled back into the hazard, and he made bogey. He had other birdie opportunities, including a six-footer at No. 17, but his putter, having spoken, evidently had no more to say. Though Nicklaus had looked relaxed during the first two rounds, his face was settling more and more into the frown that has always been his trademark in competition. He knew from long experience that he wasn't out of the tournament, but he also knew that he couldn't keep failing to capitalize on his opportunities. When the putt rimmed out of the cup at the 17th, he flinched visibly, and the energy seemed to drain out of him as he trudged off the green.

"I have a good chance with a good round tomorrow," he said as he sat on the terrace signing autographs, but he might have been the only person in Augusta who really believed that. The men ahead of him weren't all that far ahead, but they happened to be the leading golfers in the world, and Nicklaus simply had too much ground to make up. In the opinion of the astute Herbert Warren Wind, author of several golf books and coauthor, with Nicklaus, of *The Greatest Game of All*, this particular Masters had not shaped up as an opportunity for Nicklaus to win a twentieth major. Over the years, Wind has probably observed Nicklaus's game as closely as anyone, and his scenario for another Nicklaus victory required different circumstances. "I thought," Wind wrote, "that if he made the 36-hole cut in a major tournament, his extraordinary ability to compete might enable him to fight his way into contention, and, if the fourth round turned into one of those grim afternoons in which there was a general falling away of the men close to the lead, Nicklaus, with his stubborn resolution, might hold on and win. However, in the tournament I envisaged I saw him winning only because a 71 or a 70, or at the lowest, a 69, would see him through."

There is never any telling what the last round of a tournament will bring, but it was hard to imagine that the eight men ahead of Nicklaus would conveniently back up on Sunday. In fact, Wind's estimate of Nicklaus's chances was a good deal more generous than that of Ken Venturi, who had told a reporter for *USA Today* that it was time for Jack to start thinking about retirement. Other newspapers had taken up the same theme, and if Nicklaus's friend John Montgomery had clipped all the stories about the decline and fall of the Golden Bear, he wouldn't have had room to tape them to Nicklaus's refrigerator.

The golfers ahead of Nicklaus weren't worried about him, either. At dinner that night, Tom Kite and his companions had found themselves talking about Nicklaus, and Kite said, "I don't think Jack can win another Masters. I don't think he can win another *tournament.*"

### THE LEADERS AFTER 54 HOLES

| | | | | |
|---|---|---|---|---|
| Greg Norman | 70 | 72 | 68 | 210 |
| Nick Price | 79 | 69 | 63 | 211 |
| Donnie Hammond | 73 | 71 | 67 | 211 |
| Bernhard Langer | 74 | 68 | 69 | 211 |
| Seve Ballesteros | 71 | 68 | 72 | 211 |
| Tom Kite | 70 | 74 | 68 | 212 |
| Tom Watson | 70 | 74 | 68 | 212 |
| Tommy Nakajima | 70 | 71 | 71 | 212 |
| Sandy Lyle | 76 | 70 | 68 | 214 |
| Jack Nicklaus | 74 | 71 | 69 | 214 |

# 8

## Sunday

There is nothing sleepy about the city of Augusta on the Sunday of the Masters. By eight o'clock the whole place is wide awake and stirring, and as soon as people have downed their ham and grits, they get in their cars and sit in the traffic already backed up on Washington Road, the four-lane strip that provides access to most of Augusta National's parking lots. The souvenir vendors have already set up their stands, hawking their visors and caps and, it is said, hawking badges as well. The Masters does not sell day tickets but only season passes, which are good for admission throughout the week of the tournament. These badges cost $85, not that the price matters. You can't buy one from the Augusta National Golf Club, not unless you've been buying one for years, and you can't even get your name on a waiting list. The club officials closed it when it grew so long that the waiting period began to exceed an average life expectancy. If you're really desperate for a badge and have $750, you can probably find a scalper who will sell you one. Or you can join those other poor souls who line Washington Road holding up their hand-lettered signs: MASTERS TICKET WANTED. WILL PAY ANYTHING.

Nobody was giving up a badge on this particular Sunday. Long before play actually started, fans had staked out their spots around the greens and thronged those two great gathering places, Amen Corner and the shady juncture of the two par

3s, the 6th and the 16th, where a dazzling slope of azaleas was reflected in the still water of the pond that serves as the 16th fairway. The air was downright sultry and the flowers were at the peak of their brilliance. One of golf's greatest stages was set for what promised to be another stirring Masters drama.

Not only did the leader board boast the most formidable names in golf, but each one of them had a driving motivation to win this particular Masters. All alone in front was Greg Norman, still seeking his first major, the championship that would justify his Bunyanesque reputation. Ballesteros was only a shot behind him, nursing his grudge against Deane Beman and the American golf establishment, determined to make good on the prediction he'd made—or hadn't made—earlier in the week; a victory for the Spaniard would make it hard for anyone to deny that he was indeed *el major golfista del mundo.* Langer, tied with Ballesteros, had his own sights set on the number one spot, and so did Tom Watson, a shot farther back.

Nick Price would be trying to bring off one of the most difficult feats in golf: to play two career rounds back to back, and win his first major into the bargain. Tom Kite, almost overlooked in this glittering company, had quiet confidence that his game was coming to a peak; he was going to have another chance to capture the major title that had so far eluded him. Tommy Nakajima, who had made light of his own ambitions—"I used to want to win the Masters," he joked, "but now I think I would like to win all four majors"—knew that a victory in Augusta would be seen as a national triumph in Japan. Donnie Hammond would have liked nothing better than to prove that his presence on the star-studded leader board was not a fluke. And Jack Nicklaus, of course, would be mounting another effort to win his twentieth major, though his chances, and his motivation, were perhaps weakest of all. Nobody really expected him to start making putts on this Sunday, and if sheer desire had anything to do with the outcome of golf tournaments—well, how could Nicklaus, with nineteen majors to his credit, still covet another one?

In fact, this Masters was looking more and more as if it

would mark a definitive changing of the guard. Ballesteros,
Langer, Norman, and the other international players had
clearly become a force to be reckoned with. No longer were
they the challengers; they were the golfers to beat. As it happened, the pairings played up what had been for American
golf fans the most troubling theme of the tournament. In four
of the last five twosomes to tee off—Nicklaus and Lyle, Watson
and Nakajima, Kite and Ballesteros, Hammond and Langer, in
that order—an American was paired with a foreign golfer. The
last twosome, Price and Norman, was made up of two talented
foreigners.

The issue was sensitive enough to prompt Gary Player,
that veteran globe-trotter, to downplay the importance of national origin. "We're all golfers," he said, stressing the ecumen-
ical nature of the game. He was speaking to a television audi-
ence just before leaving Augusta to make the long trek home
to South Africa. But the fans pouring through the gates to
watch the final round of the tournament were very much
aware of the us-versus-them nature of the competition, and
they could hardly be blamed for hoping that an American
would give them something to cheer about.

Which American? Nicklaus got off to a promising start
when he birdied the second hole, but he promptly gave that
stroke back when he missed a four-footer and bogeyed the
fourth. Watson ran off five pars and then dropped a stroke at
the sixth. Hammond lost strokes painfully, one at a time, and
made the turn in 40—and felt just as he had on Thursday,
when he wanted to run and hide. In a sense he did hide, for
his name came down from the leader boards (and most fans
would never know that he showed his stuff on the back nine,
posting a 34). Tom Kite bogeyed the first hole—it was the third
time during the tournament he had bogeyed that innocuous-
looking par 4—but birdied the second, then turned right
around and bogeyed the third.

Kite was doing everything he could to ease himself back
into the comfortable groove he'd found on Saturday, but his
pairing with Ballesteros wasn't helping. There was no love lost

between the two men. They had been pitted against each other in the singles matches on the final day of the 1985 Ryder Cup competition, that black day for Americans, and Ballesteros, three down with five holes to play, had rallied to halve the match. Kite hadn't forgotten the unruly crowds, and the outcome of that match had left a bitter taste. Moreover, the relentless intensity that Ballesteros brings to a round is the exact opposite of the calm deliberation that Kite tries to cultivate. Temperamentally, the two men are fire and ice, and Kite was going to have to work hard to stay cool.

Jut-jawed, fidgety, dressed in the somber colors he prefers—midnight-blue pants, royal-blue shirt—and, as usual, bending his brother Vicente's ear with rapid-fire Spanish, Ballesteros nevertheless started his round with exemplary patience. He registered pars on the first six holes. Since he'd been in the spotlight all week, and since his last Masters victory, in 1983, had been secured with a flying start—he opened birdie, eagle, par, birdie, and left the field clutching air—his run of pars seemed rather tame.

But Ballesteros wasn't losing ground. Everybody else seemed to be marking time too. The only player who'd forged ahead was Langer, who got himself into a tie for the lead with a birdie at No. 2.

Otherwise, the same red numbers kept dropping into the slots beside the names of the leaders. Norman was under way with five consecutive pars, but the numbers didn't tell anything like the whole story, since he was banging the ball all over the course. His playing partner, Nick Price, had immediately sensed that Norman's adrenaline was surging. The two men were neighbors in Orlando, Florida, and Price could read Norman well enough to compare their moods when they stepped onto the first tee. After his brilliant round on Saturday, Price was keyed up, but Norman was supercharged.

"It takes a special kind of golfer to make things happen at a tournament like the Masters," Price said, "and Greg was ready to do it. He was ready to give his absolute best. When he stood on that first tee, he wasn't thinking he might hit a bad drive. He was thinking, Hey, this is Greg Norman, and I don't back off. He just wanted to crunch it out of there."

Crunch it he did, right into the trees. After scrambling to save that par, he was bunkered at No. 2, missed the green at No. 3, and hit his tee shot so far left at No. 4 that he ended up on the fifth tee—and then chipped back down to a green that sloped away from him, and saved another par. Miraculously, he was still even par for the day and still tied for the lead when he hit one of his skyscraping irons into the sixth green and knocked in a seven-footer for his birdie.

For a few minutes, he was a shot clear of the field. His lead widened to two shots over Langer, a hole ahead of him, when the West German hooked his tee shot at No. 7 and took a bogey. At the long eighth, trying to make sure he didn't hook again, Langer overcorrected and pushed his tee shot into the trees on the right. When he took a second bogey, he could say *auf wiedersehen* to his hopes of winning.

Meanwhile, Ballesteros had made his first birdie of the day at No. 7 with a drive, a pitch, and a putt. The leader board showed that the foreign players were at the top, with the veteran Americans barely staying in touch.

Then, suddenly, the tournament-within-a-tournament began. The pros are in the habit of saying that this little tournament, the real tournament, begins on Sunday at the 10th tee, but at the Fiftieth Masters it began at the 8th green. More precisely, it began in the 8th fairway, 75 yards from the hole, where Tom Kite, in the pairing ahead of Langer, hit his third shot on this uphill par 5.

Kite hit a sand wedge. The ball rose in a high parabola, skipped once on the green, took a second smaller hop, and had

| | |
|---|---|
| Norman | −7 |
| Ballesteros | −6 |
| Langer | −5 |
| Price | −5 |
| Kite | −3 |
| Watson | −3 |
| Nicklaus | −2 |

just enough steam left on it to tumble into the hole. Eagle. It was the first eagle of the tournament at No. 8, and the crowd greeted it with loud exclamations. In one sweet swoop, Kite had gone to five under and overtaken just about everyone ahead of him on the leader board.

Now Ballesteros. His expression didn't change when Kite holed out; if anything, it became more fixed and adamant, as if Kite's eagle had presented him with a challenge. He waited patiently for the applause to die out. Only 40 yards from the green, he chose to play a very different shot from Kite's, a pitch-and-run that came in low, just over the fringe, and snaked toward the pin. The goggle-eyed gallery sent up another roar when it, too, hit the flagstick and fell into the cup. Back-to-back eagles!

Instead of walking onto the green to retrieve his ball, Ballesteros made a beeline for the ninth tee. His eagle, coming right on top of Kite's, and right after the birdie at the seventh, had taken the Spaniard to eight under par and put him in the lead, one stroke ahead of Norman. Once again he was the hammer in this tournament, and as he waited for the crowd to calm down, he and Kite grinned at each other, the only smile they exchanged during the round.

The game was on, and everybody at Augusta National knew it, including Jack Nicklaus. He was standing on the ninth green, getting ready to make a birdie putt, when the first roar—the roar for Kite's eagle—backed him away from the ball. Even at a distance of some 500 yards, it was loud enough to discompose him.

By his own calculations, Nicklaus had to have this putt. He'd lined it up carefully with Jackie peering over his shoulder, the two of them disagreeing. Jackie read the 11-footer to go one way, Nicklaus Senior to go the other, and so they concluded that it was another one of those putts that nobody could read.

Considering that Nicklaus was exactly where he had started the day, two under par, and that he had already missed a pair of short putts—the tiddler at No. 4, and a slightly longer putt at No. 6 that would have converted his fine tee shot into a birdie—he was in a remarkably cheerful frame of mind. He seemed to have decided that he was going to enjoy this round, though he had by no means conceded the tournament to the younger men playing behind him. That had been clear enough at No. 8, where he reached back for a big drive—and slammed it into the pines. The safe shot would have been to play out with an iron, but Nicklaus, trailing, decided to hit a full 3-wood through a six-foot opening between two thick tree trunks; and as long as he was letting the stops out, he decided to cut it a little. If you happened to be given to understatement, you would have called it an imaginative shot. Only a man who was still determined to win the tournament would have tried to pull it off, and Nicklaus didn't get exactly the result he had anticipated. The ball came out of the trees, all right, but not through the opening he was aiming at. Instead, it sailed through a tiny gap, no more than a chink of daylight, that Nicklaus hadn't even noticed.

That little piece of luck didn't lead to a birdie, but it almost certainly prevented a bogey, and it gave the Bear's spirits a lift. He figured that he was still in this thing. In fact, he still had a number in mind. Before this round, in a phone conversation with his son Steve, Nicklaus had guessed that he would need to shoot a 65 to win this Masters, a 66 to tie, and nothing had happened to make him change his mind. Nobody had started out in a rush, and after he had pitched close at No. 9, simple arithmetic told him that he'd better close out the front nine with a birdie and a 35. To play the back nine in 30 was a tall order.

So he needed this putt. The roar for Kite's eagle had faded, and Nicklaus settled again into his putting stance, that familiar crouch that resembles a burly question mark. Before he could stroke the putt, the second roar, this one for Ballesteros, put him off. He appeared to be more amused than upset, and though it has never been his habit to speak to the gallery, he said, "Let's see if we can make a roar of our own."

When he stood over the putt a third time, and rolled it into the cup, the crowd obliged with the roar he'd requested—the affectionate, good-humored cheer that the situation called for.

Nicklaus was now three under, but the leader board visible beyond the 18th green showed that he was five strokes behind Ballesteros. It would take more than one putt to get the Olden Bear back into contention.

Nicklaus's drive at No. 10 was pushed right into the gallery, where it hit a spectator and stopped. No harm done. He hit a 4-iron to the green, 25 feet short of the pin. This was longer than any putt he'd made all week, but—who can ever say why?—he felt comfortable when he stood over it. He ran it in. Four under now, and still several shots back, but the cheers were louder than before. They weren't just pat-on-the-old-bear's-back cheers, either. They were go-get-'em cheers.

The largest gallery at the Masters is always assembled in Amen Corner, and it grew even larger as Nicklaus fans arrived with their excited tidings. A buzz spread through the crowd before Nicklaus marched over the crest of the 11th fairway, and those who didn't get the news by word-of-mouth could soon read it. On the scoreboard beyond the sentinel pond, there was a red 3, showing that Nicklaus had birdied the 9th, and a red 4, for the birdie at the 10th, fell into place just as he appeared. The board also showed that Ballesteros had dropped a stroke at the 9th (where he drove into the woods, and the ball came to rest against a pine root; not even Ballesteros, with his genius for recovery shots, could do anything with it).

When Nicklaus came into view, then, he was only three shots behind the Spaniard. With power reminiscent of his palmy days, he had driven the ball so far down the fairway that the pond didn't trouble him at all. He had only an 8-iron left to the green on this 455-yard par 4. He planted it 20 feet from the flag. Once again he saw the line of his putt, saw it exactly; it ran just inside the stud that his playing partner, Lyle, had used to mark his ball. The stud gave Nicklaus the point he needed, and the putt was in all the way.

There were hosannas in Amen Corner, where even the doubters were starting to believe. With three birdies in a row, Nicklaus had climbed right back into the tournament. He hoisted his putter, that big war club, high into the air and looked at Jackie, shaking his head, with a huge, pleased, incredulous grin. Jackie was incredulous, too, after three days of watching his father's putts miss the hole. He could tell that Nicklaus Senior was pumped up, and as for Jackie himself— he'd bounced straight up when that putt fell, as if the bent grass under him were a trampoline.

Nicklaus was not oblivious to the cheers. One of his trade- marks, of course, had always been his ability to seal himself off and focus on the matter at hand, and he made an effort to do just that when he stepped onto the 12th tee. His customary frown of concentration was in place, but he was hardly calm. On the contrary, he felt he'd better tamp down his excitement, and he chose to play a conservative tee shot. The pin was cut in its traditional fourth-round position, at the far right of the long, narrow green—the most difficult position. Nicklaus would be content to put his 7-iron in the center of the green, safely avoiding the pond in front and the traps behind and walk away with his par.

He gave the hazards a wide berth, too wide. His tee shot finished well left of the green, and then he got a pair of bad breaks. The first came when his chip shot, well struck, took a funny kick in the fringe and, instead of running down to the cup, stayed up on a little ridge above the cup. He was left with a downhill seven-footer. Directly in his line was a spike mark, with points of grass standing up like thumbtacks. When the putt rolled over them, the ball bobbled and lurched to the right—and burned the right edge of the cup.

Bogey.

Nicklaus slumped as if he'd been slugged in the solar plexus. He banged the sole of his putter down on the spike mark. It is probably just as well that very few people heard his short, choked oath. He was boiling, and not just because he'd missed the putt, or because he'd been the victim of a spike mark. What really hurt was that he'd made a bad deci- sion, a decision to play safe when every instinct cried out to go for it.

The leader board showed just how costly that bogey was. Nicklaus, with only five holes to play, still had three strokes to make up, and the men he was trying to catch, Ballesteros and Norman, were power hitters who could be expected to attack the two par 5s on the back nine.

| | |
|---|---|
| Norman | −7 |
| Ballesteros | −7 |
| Kite | −5 |
| Langer | −5 |
| Nicklaus | −4 |
| Watson | −3 |

Most of the gallery, taking in those numbers, had to conclude that the spell was broken. To see the Golden Bear get into the fray on the last round of the Masters stirred deep memories, but Nicklaus had made a similar dash yesterday, running off a string of birdies in the middle of his round. This was Sunday, and it took a blind leap of faith to believe that he could conjure up the shots he would need to catch Ballesteros.

The Spaniard, after his bogey at No. 9, had notched his pars at No. 10 and No. 11. He was holding steady at seven under par while the rest of the field fell slowly away—slowly or, in Norman's case, swiftly.

Norman's undoing came at No. 10, the scene of so many of his previous travails. This time he hooked his drive into the treetops, where it vanished with a resounding smack. The ball took its own sweet time coming down—and just when it seemed that this might be one of those tree-eats-ball stories, it popped out onto the fairway. A break for Norman, but he was still a long way from the green. He hooked his next shot, a 2-iron, and sent it bounding through the gallery (no chance of a spectator stopping this one—it had some mustard on it). It stopped close to a tree, where Norman could only jab at it, slapping it across the green and into a trap. One explosion and two putts later, he had his double bogey, and it looked as if this 10th hole—his Waterloo in 1981—was going to cost him another Masters.

At this point the golfer in the best position to press Ballesteros was Kite. He was tied with Norman at five under, but he was purring along nicely now. He'd found his groove. He was hitting the ball with complete freedom and assurance, driving it out there with Ballesteros, and nailing his irons. His approach at No. 10 was dead on the flag, but he hit a diffident putt. At No. 11, he played another superlative iron shot, giving himself a birdie putt of less than 10 feet. These two holes, the 10th and 11th, long and rigorous par 4s, are not usually considered birdie holes, but before the tournament Kite had talked strategy with Hubert Green, a player who also gives up some distance off the tee. They had agreed that the key holes for them would have to be the tough par 3s and par 4s, not the par 5s, where the Normans and Ballesteroses had an edge (though Kite was holding his own on the par 5s; he played them in 10 under par during the tournament). Here at No. 11, Kite executed that strategy perfectly, making the birdie putt. He was only one stroke back.

Both Kite and Ballesteros played the 12th as Nicklaus had, showing plenty of respect. Kite, with the honor, reproduced Nicklaus's shot almost exactly, missing the green to the left. Ballesteros came through with the shot both of them had failed to hit, dropping his 7-iron in the geometrical center of the green. He gave his brother the thumbs-up sign. In his book, this tee shot at No. 12 was the most treacherous shot on the back nine, and he was satisfied. He almost sank his 30-footer. Kite chipped 12 feet past the hole and worked hard on the putt. It fell, and a grin of relief lit up his face.

Now the 13th. Kite played a daring drive close to Rae's Creek and contoured with just the right amount of draw to get around the bend of the trees and into the level part of the fairway. Position A. Ballesteros pegged up his ball, shifted his weight around, and glared down the fairway that, the last two days, had eluded him. He'd been in the right rough both times. Today he couldn't afford a mistake, not with Kite on his heels and, after the drive he'd just hit, looking at an almost certain birdie, maybe another eagle. Furthermore, from up ahead came a volley of cheers, sending the message that Nicklaus had jumped right back in with another birdie of his own. One of the Spaniard's most vivid memories of the Masters went back to 1978, when he watched Gary Player, his playing partner, shoot a 30 on the back nine and overtake the younger golfers who had started the day well in front of him. He knew exactly what an older, experienced golfer—an experienced champion—could do over the closing holes of Augusta National. He had to figure that if he wanted this title, he would have to *win* it—and besides, it was in character for Ballesteros to win, or lose, with a bold stroke.

He gave his drive all he had. No elegant follow-through this time, but an off-balance sideways stagger. The ball split the fairway, Ballesteros didn't take his eyes off it until it was safely at rest in the short grass. As he strode toward the ball, deeply engaged in conversation with Vicente, a few members of the gallery offered suggestions about his next shot. "Hit it into the water," they said. Masters galleries are among the most mannerly in sports; they have sometimes been gently chided for their habit of applauding even the most indifferent shots. Now, though, they were letting the Spaniard know just where their loyalties stood.

Ballesteros isn't rabbit-eared. He has often said that he plays best when he feels that the crowd is against him, and the awareness that he was anything but the sentimental favorite had been with him all week. The jeers only fueled his determination to play an ideal shot—and he regarded this shot at No. 13 as the second most difficult shot on the closing holes. He was just under 200 yards from the hole. He chose his 4-iron and set up to play a soft fade.

He couldn't have hit any better. Indeed, the shot he hit looked as if it would become storied as the shot that won the Fiftieth Masters. The pin was on the right of the green, and one golfer after another had fired a long iron that came in on the correct line, checked up, and remained well short of the flag. Nicklaus had just played such a shot, and Kite's approach would also sit right down beside the dent of the ball mark. Ballesteros, however, read the speed and contour of the green perfectly. His ball released when it landed, ran almost to the back fringe, and then, just when it seemed about to expire, caught the downslope and curled slowly toward the pin as if mesmerized by it. It finished six or seven feet from the hole.

Beaming, Ballesteros shook Vicente's hand as he strode toward the green—a gesture one could only interpret as meaning that the Spaniard thought the deed was done. It is one of the oldest clichés in sport to say that he now sensed the kill, but that is exactly how he looked. He had played a full shot to a tiered green with more imagination and finesse than most golfers could have played a chip shot, and it was unthinkable that he should miss the putt. He didn't. He rolled it into the center of the cup for his second eagle of the day and what looked like an ironclad lead. He had gone to nine under par, and he was playing with radiant confidence, coming through with the inspired shot when he needed it.

When Shakespeare's Glendower boasted that he could summon spirits from the vasty deep, Hotspur replied, "Why, so can I, or so can any man; But will they come when you do call them?"

Twice now Ballesteros had summoned the spirits—and they had come both times.

The Spaniard's brilliance put a momentary damper on the crowd. To win his third green jacket, it seemed, he had only to play the finishing holes without mishap. The real suspense appeared to be in the battle for second place. Kite, having made his birdie at No. 13, remained two behind Ballesteros. Norman was three behind, and Tom Watson was suddenly making a move; he had gone to five under par with consecutive birdies at No. 13 and No. 14.

Still farther up the course, Corey Pavin streaked into the picture just as he had yesterday, with an eagle at the 15th. He'd smacked another 4-wood onto the green, but this time he had to hole a 25-footer for his eagle. Six under par when he went to the tee at No. 16, he conformed to pattern and played this hole just as he had on Saturday—by dumping his tee shot into the lake. Repetition is a comic device, they say, but tell that to Corey Pavin; he found no humor whatsoever in his misfortune. Without even waiting for the ball to splash down, he walked back to the bench at the rear of the tee, sat down, and buried his face in his hands.

Jack Nicklaus, at five under, was looking as if he might have to settle for third or fourth place. He needed birdies, but he parred the 14th. At No. 15 he hit a big drive, sending the ball down the right center of the fairway to the bottom of the

area mounded with those humps known as "chocolate drops."
After checking his yardage—as many times as he has played
Augusta National, he still carries a yardage book in his back
pocket, and he still uses it—he calculated that he was 214 yards
from the pin. If he wanted to get back into the tournament—
and he still hadn't conceded anything—he absolutely had to
have an eagle here.

He asked Jackie for a 4-iron, and Jackie thought to himself,
*That's a* big *4-iron.* But he didn't question his father's judgment.

"How far do you think an eagle would go?" Nicklaus
asked.

"Let's see it," replied Jackie.

Nicklaus got all of that 4-iron. The ball fell in from right
to left, stitching the flagstick. It came within a few feet of going
into the cup on the fly. Nicklaus pumped both fists into the air;
from the cheers he knew that he was close, but he didn't know
how close. Jackie saw it, all right, but Nicklaus Senior couldn't
see that far. He'd always been color-blind, and in recent years
his vision had dimmed so that he no longer had the pleasure
of seeing his ball finish.

He set out for the green in his determined walk, straining
forward, but he kept saluting the crowd. Not too many years
ago, he would have acknowledged their cheers in a more per-
functory way, zeroed in on the task before him. It was clear,
though, that he savored this ovation, and he had to make an
effort to get down to work. He labored over the 12-footer,
banishing all the excuses he could give himself for missing
it—he was forty-six years old, he was too far behind, he'd already made his share of putts today, this particular putt had a
nasty break in it. No one could really blame him if he missed,
and as a matter of fact, he had missed an identical putt on this
green once before, in 1975, when he hit it too gently. How he
could remember that putt of eleven years ago is a matter for
students of the cerebral cortex, but remember it he did—and
he didn't make the same mistake. This putt he rapped firmly,
and it was in all the way.

Pandemonium!

Every veteran of golf tournaments develops an ear for the noises of the gallery, from the merely polite rustle of applause for a par to the drawn-out sigh that swells in volume as a long birdie putt rolls toward the cup, and explodes in a roar when it falls—or ends in a collective groan when it misses. There is a perceptible difference, too, between the cheers for a birdie that is well earned—like the birdie Nicklaus made at the ninth—and the enthusiastic yells and shrieks for a shot that may affect the outcome of a tournament. A decisive eagle is in a special category, and when that eagle happens to be made by a forty-six-year-old Jack Nicklaus and brings him to the brink of winning his sixth Masters and his twentieth major championship—well, that roar was historic.

The Fiftieth Masters had just kicked into another dimension. All golf fans believe in miracles, and the thousands crowded into the vicinity of the 15th green were convinced that nothing less than a miracle was in the making. As for the miracle worker, Nicklaus, he had rejoiced when the ball fell into the cup, but he was now standing quietly at the edge of the green, blinking back the tears that had welled up. His emotions had never been so visible on a golf course.

The crowd was in a state between frenzy and exaltation, and it was growing every second. People were streaming toward the 15th hole from all over the course. They had come to watch a drama, but what was unfolding now hovered on the threshold of legend. That huge cheer had made the workers in the concession stands abandon their posts, and the fans who'd already started toward the exits, thinking Ballesteros had the tournament sewed up, stopped in their tracks, made an about-face, and hightailed it back toward the source of the noise. Back on the 14th tee, Nick Price and Greg Norman looked at each other and shook their heads; they'd never heard a roar like that. "All Greg and I knew," Price said, "was that something astonishing was happening, but we had no idea what it was."

Nicklaus moved to the 16th tee, reminding himself that he had three tough holes left to play. He took his time over his tee shot; he didn't like the look of the spot where he first teed up, and moved the ball a few feet. Two strokes behind Ballesteros, he realized that he still needed birdies, and the 16th was a hole where he had picked up several. He birdied it during the final round in 1963, the year he won his first Masters, and he birdied it again in 1975, the year he won his fifth Masters. Now, seeking his sixth title, he nearly aced it. His 5-iron landed a few feet above the hole, turned over, and rolled toward the hole. The thousands who could see the ball—and millions more watching on television—held their breath as it drifted toward the cup, missing by inches. Nicklaus, of course, had to wait until he approached the green, walking the length of the lake with a wall of jubilant fans on either side, before he could see how close he'd put it.

The vast gallery was so quiet that you could hear the birds peeping in the trees when Nicklaus finally addressed that short putt, and there was another seismic cheer when it fell. Nicklaus gave Jackie an odd smile, as if to say, "Even I don't believe I'm doing this."

Through all the uproar, Tom Kite was unruffled. He kept right on playing superior golf, taking the calculated risks he had to take. At the 14th he was longer off the tee than Ballesteros, and he lofted a high approach that came in exactly where it had to, inches behind the back of that high crest that runs across the front of the green. Both Ballesteros and Nicklaus had made sure they cleared the crest, and both found themselves on the back fringe. Kite, though, had a real crack at still another birdie. He went carefully through his putting routine, taking two smooth practice strokes before he set up over the ball, trying to establish precisely the right speed for his stroke. But, as he had done on his birdie attempt at No. 10, he left the ball short.

Ballesteros still held a two-shot lead over Kite and Nicklaus. When he came striding over the hill on the 15th fairway— he had launched another huge drive—he knew exactly where he stood in relation to his nearest competitors. Nicklaus was just playing the 16th, and Watson was just arriving at the 15th green, where he'd given himself an opportunity for an eagle. No matter what glories Ballesteros had envisioned for himself, they could hardly have equaled the scene that spread itself out before him. Here he was with a third Masters within reach, and this time he would prevail against the two greatest American players. The sight of Watson pursuing Nicklaus was familiar enough, but Ballesteros had both of them in his sights. His campaign to establish himself as the premier golfer of his own generation had brought him to this decisive moment when he could prove to the golfing world that he had surpassed the two men who had ruled before him.

As Watson prepared to putt for his eagle, he kept peering anxiously toward the 16th green. He didn't want to be in midstroke when Nicklaus cashed in his birdie and sent another wave of noise crashing over the course. This was a makable putt, a putt that could take Watson to seven under, and put him, momentarily, into a tie with Nicklaus. He was in precisely the same situation Nicklaus had been in minutes before, and if he eagled . . . but he hurried his stroke. The putt never had a chance, and Watson watched it peter out with the rueful expression of a man who has just spilled his drink at his feet. His challenge had ended.

Then it was Tommy Nakajima's turn to crane toward the 16th green. He was on his way to a respectable round of 72 and a tie for eighth place in the tournament, but he was frankly overwhelmed by what was happening all around him. He would say later, "I was just happy to be there."

Ballesteros waited. He waited for the roar for Nicklaus—he was only one shot ahead now—and waited for Watson and Nakajima to finish out their birdies. He watched Kite put his long approach safely on the 15th green. His turn now, and he was still debating between a hard 5-iron and an easy 4-iron. A birdie here, on the hole he'd birdied yesterday, and eagled the day before, and he was home free.

He chose the 4-iron, the club he'd used at No. 13, and set up as if he meant to play the same kind of shot, a shot that would fade slightly as it came into the flag. Something went drastically wrong. Ballesteros, the man who usually flows through the ball with such classic grace, turned his body much too quickly and made a lurching, slapping, ugly swing. He simply threw the clubhead at the ball, hitting it fat and with the clubface closed.

There was an eerie roar, half groan and half cheer, as the ball streaked in a low hook toward the pond. Some people in the bleachers behind the Sarazen Bridge began chanting, "U. S. A., U. S. A., U. S. A.," and others, pulling for Nicklaus, were nevertheless stunned by the calamity that had opened the door for him. Ballesteros hadn't lost the tournament, not yet, but everyone sensed that what had just taken place was—if any misfortune on a golf course deserved the word—a tragedy.

Ballesteros conferred with an official and went about the business of playing out the hole. He took his drop and played a full wedge to the green, exactly on line but a little strong. He missed the putt. Bogey.

Kite picked up his birdie, and there was a three-way tie for the lead.

As he set up to play his drive at the 17th, Nicklaus heard that strange roar in back of him, and stepped away from his ball. He thought that Seve had either hit it stiff or hit it into the water, but he didn't ask which. He didn't want any distractions. He still had two holes to play, and he was going to play them with every ounce of concentration. Knowing that the pin was in the back right of the 17th green, he wanted to draw his tee shot to the left side of the fairway, giving himself the best possible angle to the flag.

He overdid it. The ball turned too much and finished off the fairway, on hard ground beneath two pines. The tree trunks weren't in his way, but the overhanging limbs were. He was 120 yards from the green, one of the firmest greens at

| Nicklaus | −8 |
| Ballesteros | −8 |
| Kite | −8 |
| Norman | −6 |
| Watson | −6 |

Augusta National, but he was going to have to play a low shot. He set up with the ball farther back in his stance than usual. Using a wedge, he nipped it out of its tight lie and sent it skimming just under the pine branches. With the heavy backspin he'd put on it, the ball skidded as soon as it pitched onto the green and rolled to a stop 11 feet from the hole.

Nicklaus wasted no time trying to follow the flight of the ball. The spectators had started to bolt toward the green, and their boisterous reactions were beginning to concern him a little. Even though he was convoyed from the 16th green to the 17th tee by an escort of gallery marshals, the crowds had swarmed all over him, yelling and hooting and banging him on the back, and while he appreciated the fact that they were trying to urge him on, he also felt that he'd better protect himself. He made a speedy escape back to the safety of the fairway, handed Jackie his wedge, and took the big aluminum putter that was fast becoming the most famous club since White Fang, the stick he used the last time he put aside his old blade. White Fang made the putts that won the 1967 U.S. Open at Baltusrol.

This putt was for the lead. Jackie read it as a double-breaker that would tail off to the right, but Nicklaus, drawing once again on years of experience, thought it would hold a straighter line. He knew he was right when the ball was still three feet from the hole, and he took a giant step forward, holding the putter up like a torch.

Jackie was airborne again, and members of the gallery were shaking their fists and giving each other high fives. When he removed the ball from the cup, Nicklaus rolled his eyes heavenward as if in thanks, and he stopped at the side of the green to fight back more tears.

One more hole. Nicklaus collected himself for this last tee shot, a hard 3-wood tailor-made to follow the left-to-right turn of the uphill 18th fairway. The pin was on the top shelf of the tiered green; Nicklaus hit a 5-iron that encountered a fitful breeze and didn't make it to the top. Still, after striding up the fairway through another continuous and ecstatic ovation, he almost dropped the 40-footer he'd left himself. When he tapped in for his par, he'd brought in the round he had to have—35 out, 30 in, for the 65 he thought would win.

He shook hands with Sandy Lyle and started to shake hands with Jackie—but that handshake turned into a spontaneous hug. An old saying has it that a golfer is alone on the course with his shot and his God, but Jackie's presence throughout this round had somehow helped to make the galleries feel they had shared intimately in the emotions. "Dad, watching you play today was the thrill of my life," Jackie said, and father and son left the green with their arms draped over each other's shoulders.

Nicklaus's closing surge had been so dramatic that it was hard to realize that the tournament wasn't over. These last few holes had had an air of triumph about them and the grandeur of a Hollywood epic—but Hollywood would have seen to it that the movie ended when the hero performed his last deed, and we would have had our last sight of him as the worshipful multitudes rushed to raise him aloft.

As matters stood, though, Nicklaus signed his scorecard and was hustled away by green-jacketed Masters officials to a nearby cabin, the Bob Jones Cabin, to sweat out the rest of the tournament. Ballesteros and Kite still had a chance to tie him. Both men had parred the 16th, and at the 17th, the Spaniard had a long birdie putt. He gave it a chance—and when the ball ran by the cup, he waved as if he didn't care whether it ever stopped running.

He took scarcely any time over the next putt, knocking it back in the general direction of the hole. It was clear enough that he merely wanted to play out the round and put an end to this ordeal. It was less clear how he felt about the crowd. He responded to their cheers—sympathetic cheers now, and tinged with guilt—after he bogeyed the 17th and trudged up the final fairway. Waving his visor and mustering a smile, he blew kisses at the gallery. You might have thought that he was expressing gratitude—but on second thought, he might just as easily have been expressing the opposite. He had to be suffering. For the first time in his career, he had thrown away a major championship that had been his to win.

Kite, meanwhile, never faltered. He parred the 17th and gave himself every chance to make the birdie he needed at No. 18, playing another fine approach shot that landed in the right fringe and kicked toward the hole. He had a 12-footer to tie Nicklaus.

This putt, the biggest putt of his life, would put him into a playoff with Nicklaus. He didn't hurry it. He took his two practice strokes before settling into his stance. The ball started out toward the heart of the cup. For 11 feet it looked as if it would fall, but in the last few inches it slowed down, curled like a pig's tail, and quivered to a halt on the rim of the cup.

Kite sank into a deep crouch as if the pressure of his terrific bid had finally descended on him. "I made that putt," he would say afterward, "it just didn't go in. I made it so many times in the practice rounds—six or seven times—and it never broke left once."

There was only one challenger left, Greg Norman. After his double bogey at the 10th and the sensational eagles by Ballesteros and Nicklaus, Norman was the forgotten man in the tournament, seemingly too far behind to get back into the lead he'd held at the start of the day. The gallery had deserted him, all but a corporal's guard, but he had no intention of simply following the cheers to the clubhouse. "Let's make something happen," he said to Price as they played the 14th.

He got his birdie there, and added another at the 15th, where he was on in two and down in two. He fired his tee shot into the green at No. 16 and let it come back down toward the hole; like Nicklaus, he missed a hole-in-one by inches.

Hot on the Bear's tracks, Norman hooked his tee shot at No. 17, and his pursuit seemed to come to an abrupt end. The ball was perched on a sprinkler head just off the 7th green, and while he could get relief from the sprinkler head, there was no relief from the pines—the same pines that Nicklaus had been under half an hour earlier. They were directly between him and the flag on the 17th green. Norman didn't have a shot, at least not what an ordinary golfer would consider a shot. But using a 5-iron, he threaded the ball between the trees, keeping it underneath the branches. He also cut it so that the ball bent toward the flag. It bounded in the fairway, just missed the edge of a bunker—in baseball it would have been called a "seeing-eye single"—and finished pin-high. Norman flashed the putt into the cup.

He'd reeled off four birdies in a row, and he was dead even with Nicklaus. When the red 9 went up on the scoreboard beside his name, some people began hotfooting it toward the 10th fairway, where a playoff would begin. In the Bob Jones Cabin, Nicklaus got down on the floor and did a few exercises to keep his back loose.

Norman split the fairway with his drive at the last hole. He was feeling confident, and he set up to play the same kind of approach that Ballesteros had attempted at No. 15. Coincidentally—or not so coincidentally, if you suspect, as Jones did, that the outcome of a golf tournament is predestined—he was swinging a 4-iron, the same club that Ballesteros had used (and the same club that Nicklaus had hit at the 15th). The swing Norman made even resembled the Spaniard's, for he spun too quickly, turning his body well before his club started down. The difference was that Norman never got his hands into the swing at all, and he pushed it deep into the gallery at the right of the green. One glance told Norman everything he needed to know, and his chin dropped to his chest.

A par was still possible, but Norman looked defeated while the gallery guards moved the crowd back and began to pick up the green beverage cups that littered the ground. Norman himself tossed a few cups aside, but this certainly wasn't the way he'd envisioned completing his round. He'd had a birdie in mind, his fifth birdie in a row—that would have been the dashing way to win his first major. "I let my ego get the best of me," he said by way of explaining his approach shot.

His chip curled onto the back on the green, about 15 feet from the hole. Nobody watched the ensuing putt with more interest than Jack Nicklaus, and when it rolled past the cup without touching it, he had won the Fiftieth Masters.

*  *  *

It had been a momentous day. Thousands of fans began to make their way slowly toward the exits, their voices still bubbling with excitement as they tried to describe the spectacular shots they'd seen, and the emotions they'd felt as the plot unfolded. They all knew they'd just seen a thriller, a tournament that would be remembered and discussed for years to come. There were rebel yells and more high fives and happy outbursts everywhere, as fans congratulated themselves on having had the good fortune to be present at Augusta National when the Golden Bear played what even he called the finest golf of his career. His 30 on the back nine had tied the course record, and his scorecard is something to behold:

444 443 453 – 35
334 443 234 – 30 – 65

To translate those numbers into words, he had played the last ten holes birdie, birdie, birdie, bogey, birdie, par, eagle, birdie, birdie, par. In the seventeen major championships he had previously won as a professional, he had never traveled at such a scorching pace over the closing holes.

The formal presentation took place on the practice green, where thousands more, reluctant to leave the scene, had gathered for one last glimpse of the champion. He was escorted onto the green by a squad of Pinkertons, and handed a microphone by Hord Hardin, the tournament chairman. "You all have been just fantastic," Nicklaus said. "Coming down the stretch was an experience I'll never forget. I've had it a couple of times in my life"—here he had to pause to get control of his voice—"I was fortunate enough to have it in '78 at St. Andrews, and in '80 at Baltusrol. I had tears in my eyes, and I had to keep saying to myself, 'Come on, Jack, you've got more golf to play.'"

Nicklaus had tears in his eyes again, and they stayed there as Bernhard Langer helped him into his sixth green jacket.

\* \* \*

His day was not yet done. When the ceremony was over, Nicklaus went to the interview room, accompanied by members of his family—his wife, Barbara; his mother, Helen; and his sister, Marilyn. Their presence brought home just how much care Nicklaus has always taken to make sure that his family gets its share of recognition. At the beginning of his career, he never failed to mention his debt to his father, Charles Nicklaus, who got him started in golf. Now the father of five children, Nicklaus said, "My kids keep me playing golf." He explained that they were always after him to take the clubs out of the closet and get out on the course. He had special praise for Jackie and the way he'd encouraged him throughout the week. "He was always telling me, 'Let's get this birdie,' 'Hold your head still on this putt,' and things like that." He talked about how Jackie had worked on his own short game with Chi Chi Rodriguez and passed on those tips to him. He mentioned the work he'd done with Jack Grout—Grout had been his teacher, and Nicklaus had always gone back to him when he needed help—after his poor showing in the Doral Open.

Then Tom McCollister entered the room, the reporter from the Atlanta *Journal* who had prophesied that Nicklaus was through. That article had been staring at Nicklaus from the refrigerator all week long. After a moment of uneasy silence, McCollister said, "Glad I could help, Jack."

Nicklaus laughed along with everyone else and then went on to say that while he'd been struggling with his game, he had promised himself not to retire from golf on a low note. Anticipating the next question, he added, "I'm not retiring now, guys. I'm not that smart."

The interview continued for almost an hour. The writers scribbled away on their notepads, trying to figure out how they could possibly file a story that would do justice to the day's events. There was too much to tell—too many shots when the outcome of the tournament hung in the balance, too many stunning reversals of fortune. And somehow or other you had to reckon with the fact that Jack Nicklaus had now won twenty major championships, a figure that conjured up the dimensions of his epic career. The young Jack Nicklaus, growing up, had known only one golf statistic, the most important golf statistic—that Bobby Jones had won thirteen majors. For several generations to come, young golfers will learn that Jack Nicklaus won twenty major championships—unless, of course, he happens to win another.

# 9

# The Once and Future Nicklaus

Golf was front-page news in papers all over the world on the day after the Fiftieth Masters. It had been a landmark tournament, one that every follower of the sport could appreciate as a masterpiece of shot-making and mounting suspense. From start to finish, it had been clear that this Masters was a contest of pride, and day after day it had brought out the best in the best golfers in the world. Everything about the tournament was writ large, as if the gods of golf had decided that it was time for another demonstration that the game is played not merely with an assortment of clubs and a small white ball; it is played with nerve, and heart, and desire.

There had never been a more emotional Masters. Golf fans—and plenty of others who don't know a bogey from a brassie—were moved by Nicklaus's victory. The sterling performances of old champions are always greeted with special applause, since they seem to make the years fall away; but for days after the tournament, for months afterward, people were still talking about Nicklaus's victory in the Fiftieth Masters with a mixture of awe and fondness. The awe was something that Nicklaus had often inspired, but the fondness was not.

Everybody knows that Nicklaus had the bad luck to begin his career when Arnold Palmer was one of the most universally admired figures in any sport. Even before he turned professional, Nicklaus ran up against Palmer in a major championship, the 1960 U.S. Open at Cherry Hills, Colorado. In those days, the top amateurs often held their own against the professionals, and Nicklaus was the reigning amateur champion, a pudgy twenty-year-old boy wonder with a big, big game.

The Cherry Hills Open is best remembered for Palmer's heroics on the front nine of the final round. He started out by driving the green on the first hole, a 346-yard par 4, and just kept pouring it on, running off six birdies in seven holes, bogeying the next one, and still making the turn in 30. His burst, however, had not scattered the field. He had started out seven strokes off the pace, and this was one of those free-for-all Opens; there were no fewer than ten other players who still had a real crack at winning the championship.

· One of them was Jack Nicklaus. He'd done some sizzling of his own on the front nine, going out in 32. For one hole he actually held the lead, a stroke in the clear, but two consecutive three-putts dropped him back into a tie, first with Palmer and then with his forty-eight-year-old playing partner, Ben Hogan, who was making his own bid to win an unprecedented fifth Open. The pressure ought to have bowled Nicklaus over, but it didn't; he finished second in that Open, two strokes behind Palmer, and Hogan said, "He would have won by five strokes if he'd had me to do his thinking for him."

Nicklaus hadn't quite arrived, not yet, but in the minds of golf fans, most of whom were Palmer worshipers, he was on a collision course with Arnie. People could identify with Palmer, who threw himself into the game heart and soul and lived out just about everybody's fantasies, but who could identify with Nicklaus? He was too young, too deliberate, and too bland. Palmer communicated his full-blooded emotions to a gallery, and even Hogan, whom Palmer had replaced at the top of the heap, had radiated the hard blue glow of high purpose. He might retreat into some remote citadel of concentration during a round of golf, but what came across to anyone following the dispatches from the kingdom of golf was an implacable passion for excellence. No doubt Nicklaus shared this, just as he shared Hogan's ability to insulate himself; but instead of passion, he conveyed only an icy calculation.

That fall Nicklaus created another big stir when the World Amateur Team Championship was played at the Merion Cricket Club, just outside Philadelphia. His four-round total of 269—66–67–68–68—was 13 strokes lower than the runner-up's (and the runner-up, incidentally, was Deane Beman). What was even more phenomenal about that score was that it was 18 strokes better than the total Ben Hogan had posted at Merion ten years earlier, when he won the 1950 U.S. Open.

Coming on top of his performance at Cherry Hills, that display at Merion put Nicklaus in the spotlight as no amateur has been since. He was being hailed as the greatest amateur since Bobby Jones, and the next spring, he was billed as the first ever who had a real chance to win the Masters and the first since John Goodman, in 1933, to win the Open. As it turned out, he tied for seventh at Augusta and played well enough at the Open to get himself within one shot of the lead during the final round. Not bad for a newly married twenty-one-year-old who was still trying to finish his college degree at Ohio State, and whose wife was expecting their first child.

Nicklaus rounded out the summer season by winning his second U.S. Amateur at Pebble Beach, demolishing his opponents in his last two matches; he won the semifinal 9 and 8, the final 8 and 6. There was nothing left for him to accomplish as an amateur, not unless he decided to model his career after that of Bobby Jones, retaining his amateur status and taking on the pros on their own terms. The idea appealed to him. Nicklaus revered Jones, and as he wrote in his memoir, *The Greatest Game of All,* his ambition had always been to see how close he could come to matching Jones's record. By this time, though, his first son had been born, and he decided he could be a better provider as a professional golfer than as an insurance salesman. That he hesitated even for a moment speaks volumes about the uncertainty of the professional tour in those days—and the career of Jack Nicklaus is one reason that it has become vastly more lucrative since then.

He turned pro for the 1962 season. Even though he didn't make the expected splash in his first few months, he was hitting his stride by the time the Open rolled around. That year

the Open was being played at Oakmont, just outside Pitts-
burgh and not far from Palmer's hometown of Latrobe, Penn-
sylvania. It was destined to become the showdown between
the immovable object and the irresistible force, between the
Titanic and the iceberg. Palmer, of course, was the Titanic,
brightly bedecked and apparently unsinkable. He had already
won a handful of tournaments that spring, including the Masters; he was working on another bid for the Grand Slam, and
during the first two rounds of the Open, paired with Nicklaus,
he was spurred on by thousands of charter members of Arnie's
Army.

Those hometown fans weren't shy, either, about letting
Nicklaus know just what they thought of him. He heard all the
familiar jeers and nicknames—Fat Jack and Ohio Fats and
Nick Louse—and though he didn't utter a word of complaint,
then or later, the hostility must have shaken him a little. If you
subscribe to the notion that the hardest steel is forged in the
hottest fire, it is reasonable to speculate that the derisive fans
contributed to the famous Nicklausian ability to shut himself
off from all distractions; in retrospect, you might even speculate that his slow and deliberate play was a way of responding
to the crowds, a way of saying, "Go ahead, let me have it—
you're not going to faze me."

At the halfway mark of the Open, Nicklaus had fallen
three shots behind Palmer. He gained a shot on him in the first
of the two Saturday rounds, and the final 18 holes turned into
a two-man contest. Nicklaus won it, 71 to 73. On Sunday there
was an 18-hole playoff, a head-to-head battle that put golf fans
into a state of exalted expectation. The case couldn't have been
stated any more clearly and starkly; the script was exactly what
any Palmer fan would have written. However, this script
called for Nicklaus to get his comeuppance, and it was Palmer
who fell behind at the start, losing four shots in 6 holes. Nicklaus held on to that lead, even when a Palmer charge whittled
it down to a single stroke. Then it was Palmer who cracked,
three-putting for a bogey at the 13th (Nicklaus had only *one*
three-putt green in the 90 holes of the tournament). They
matched pars until the 18th, where Palmer missed the green

and ran his recovery shot well past the hole. Nicklaus shot a 71, Palmer a 74, and there was no joy in Latrobe.

Nicklaus had arrived in a big way, but he had also arrived too soon—too soon, at least, for the public to accept him. He ran into surly crowds again the next spring at the Masters, and again he silenced them by winning the tournament and disposing of another redoubtable champion, Sam Snead. He seemed altogether oblivious to the pressures of tournament golf, and his bulky form, his frown—one of his most celebrated remarks in those early years was that he frowned because it required fewer facial muscles than a smile—and his outthrust jaw were soon among the most familiar sights on the tour. That broad, solid jaw is what stood out, preceding him like the cowcatcher of a steam locomotive; and indeed he gave a pretty fair approximation of a locomotive as he marched straight up a fairway, his arms held a little out at his sides, leaning slightly forward as if pulling a long train behind him. No golfer wanted to get stalled on the tracks with his mule and wagon when the Golden Bear Limited came roaring along.

Of course, he wasn't the Golden Bear, not yet. He hadn't shed those other nicknames. One by one the sportswriters were climbing aboard the train, since they had realized that Nicklaus was going to win everything there was to win; and there came to be a more or less standard Nicklaus profile, an *apologia,* that tried to explain him to a dubious and reluctant public. It wasn't just that he beat Palmer and Snead and everyone else on a regular basis; it was the way he beat them, coldly and efficiently, without any outward show of nerves or emotion or, when the task was completed, any sign of elation. True, he did occasionally send his porkpie hat skimming through the air like a Frisbee, but he collected his tournament victories as impassively as another man might collect stamps or snuffboxes. One of the obvious contradictions about this prodigious young athlete was that while he thrived on drama and created it all around him, he appeared to be the least dramatic of men.

Nicklaus never made any secret of the fact that the tournaments he most wanted to win were the major championships. He might have become a professional, but he was still measuring himself against Jones. "Practically from the time I took up the game, I knew one golf statistic cold," he wrote in his memoir. "Bob Jones had won thirteen major championships over an eight-year span." To make one more retrospective speculation, it may have been that grandiose ambition that made Nicklaus seem so remote and distant; he always knew that he was working on something big, and he was determined not to let anything stand in his way. It was no wonder that, to the galleries who saw him play, he seemed rather like Harry Vardon had to the young Bobby Jones: "He seemed to be playing something I couldn't see, which kept him serious and sort of far away from the gallery and even from his big partner; he seemed to be playing against something or someone not in the match at all. . . ."

Whatever he had in mind, Nicklaus's detachment set him apart, and his emphatic victories in the early and mid-1960s made him golf's equivalent of the New York Yankees. He was the golfer you loved to hate, and when he was on his game, he simply overpowered the opposition. He won his first PGA Championship in 1963, and though he didn't win any majors in 1964, he was the runner-up in three of them. He won his second Masters in 1965, with rounds of 67, 71, 64, and 69. The round of 64 tied the single-round record, and the four-round total of 271 eclipsed Hogan's mark by three strokes. Nicklaus had hit the ball so far off the tee during his round of 64 that to reach Augusta National's par 4s he had used his wedge five times, his 8-iron three times, his 7-iron once, and his 6-iron once. He also reached three of the par 5s in two, getting home with a 3-iron at the 8th, an uphill pull of 535 yards, and with the 5-iron at the 13th and 15th. At the presentation ceremony, Bob Jones was as much in awe as anyone else. "Jack is playing an entirely different game," he said, "a game I'm not even familiar with."

He won the Masters again in 1966, the only man ever to defend his title successfully, and later that summer at Muirfield, he won his first British Open, completing his career Grand Slam, a victory in all four of the major championships.

Only three other players had ever managed that—Gene Sarazen, Ben Hogan, and Gary Player. He now had eight majors to his credit, and his record of victories, his uncomplaining persistence, and his colossal power off the tee were changing the landscape of professional golf. It was still difficult to warm up to Nicklaus, but even the most laggard golf enthusiasts were forced to recognize the vast design that was beginning to emerge. Nobody knew how long Nicklaus's career might last, but if it kept on at the present rate, he would soon overtake the only men ahead of him on the championship ledger. He now had his own galleries, Nicklaus's Navy—though, somehow, the name never quite caught hold. Arnie was Arnie, a guy you knew on a first-name basis, but Nicklaus was Nicklaus, a man nobody really seemed to know.

Nicklaus made it easier for fans to accept him in 1969, when he decided to go on a diet. His weight had gone up to 210 pounds, but in just a few weeks he brought it down to 190. The belly was gone, and so was the extra fold around his chin and neck. He let his hair grow out, in the fashion of the day, and he dressed more stylishly—though anything would have been more stylish than his old costume of porkpie hat, baggy pants, and clinging shirts. This transformation of his image was, like every other move he made, reported in considerable detail. He had decided to lose weight, and he did his usual thoroughgoing job. Years before, he had given up smoking on the golf course when he saw a film of himself, cigarette dangling from his mouth, and this new, revised, slimmed-down Nicklaus, now the Golden Bear, seemed to be another such triumph of willpower.

The rise in his popularity, however, rested on something more than packaging. A turning point came in 1972, when he won both the Masters and the U.S. Open, the first two legs of the Grand Slam. If anyone had the talent, the stamina, and the sheer will to win that might carry off the Grand Slam, it was surely Nicklaus. His U.S. Open victory, coincidentally, was his thirteenth major, and he had drawn even with Jones on that count; he would pass him with a win at Muirfield, where the

1972 British Open was to be played. In addition, he had won the last major of 1971, the PGA, and if he could win at Muirfield, he would hold all four major titles simultaneously. That wasn't a calendar Grand Slam, but it was the next thing to it. No one could now fail to appreciate the immense scope of his ambition and talent, and if you cared for golf, if you felt any interest at all in knowing just what might be accomplished at the highest levels of the sport—well, you had to hope that Nicklaus could pull off the Slam.

At Muirfield he started cautiously, using his driver only five times in his first round. His winning strategy over this same track in 1966 had been to keep the ball in play, and he stuck to it. At the end of two rounds, he was at 142, only a stroke behind the leaders, Lee Trevino and Tony Jacklin. Then, on the third round, Trevino got hot and shot a five under par 66 while Nicklaus remained at level par.

He had six strokes to make up on the final day, and he unlimbered his driver. He got four of those strokes back on the front nine. When he birdied the 10th hole, he was a stroke ahead of Trevino, two ahead of Jacklin. Then, as he walked up the 11th fairway, the Scots greeted Nicklaus with a cheer of a kind he'd never heard before, a cheer of ringing encouragement, and he responded as he never had before, with tears.

By his own account, it was the first time he'd ever been so moved on a golf course. Nobody else saw those tears, and if they had, they probably would have supposed—Nicklaus had such a visor for a face—that he'd gotten a gnat in his eye. Nicklaus just didn't seem to feel things as other golfers did. Rather, he didn't seem to take much joy in winning. Though he never sulked when he lost, or blamed his luck, or second-guessed himself, it didn't take any special insight to know that he felt his losses, and felt them keenly. You only had to observe the all-out effort he made every time he played golf—an effort to hit every shot as well as he could, an effort to win.

Nicklaus lost at Muirfield. He was gracious in defeat—no one in the sport has ever been more gracious—and now, golf fans sympathized. It would be another irony of his career that this player of overwhelming talents would somehow be more moving in defeat, that he would win his greatest popularity when he also lost his place at the top to Watson.

In the meantime, throughout the 1970s, Nicklaus rolled on like a force of nature. If golf fans couldn't exactly identify with him—how do you identify with someone so superior and so immune to the vicissitudes that seem to beset other golfers?—they had to admit that he enlarged everyone's concept of the game. Month in and month out, year in and year out, he demonstrated exactly what it took to dominate in a game where domination ought to be impossible.

As Nicklaus himself has often pointed out, a golfer, even a great golfer, is doing well if he can win one out of every five tournaments he enters. In tennis, by contrast, a dominating player ought to win nine out of every ten matches he plays. It sometimes seemed that Nicklaus won every time he teed it up, but in fact he won only about one out of every five majors he entered. Only!

The majors are the golfing equivalents of the Golden Fleece, the goal of a mythic and fabulous quest. To capture even one is, for most golfers, the capstone of a career. To win two is to approach the company of the greats, and with three a golfer begins to make his reservation to be seated with the immortals. To win twenty is astonishing, although—yet another Nicklausian paradox—Nicklaus has always discussed his victories in the most matter-of-fact way.

He won eighteen of those major championships as a professional. That is the most monumental record in the sport, and the second most monumental, in some opinions, also belongs to Nicklaus—his record as a runner-up in the majors. He has finished second almost as often as he has finished first, nineteen times. If you start to count his other top ten finishes in the majors, you quickly encounter other astonishing facts: In the years between Nicklaus's two British Open victories, the first in 1970 and the second in 1978, he finished lower than tenth in only two majors. *Two.* During that eight-year span, he played in thirty-two major championships, won seven of them, finished second in six others, third five times, and fourth four times.

Spiritually, then, Nicklaus was the defending champion in every major that was played. It is a slight exaggeration, but only slight, to say that you had to beat the Golden Bear in order to win a major tournament.

Nicklaus didn't lack for challengers. The top golfers of the seventies—Lee Trevino, Johnny Miller, Hale Irwin, Tom Weiskopf, Ray Floyd—all had their bouts with him. To defeat Nicklaus, it goes without saying, added immeasurably to any player's stature; a golfer could make his reputation by standing up to a Nicklaus charge in a major championship. *Charge* is a word that came into the vocabulary of golf with Arnold Palmer, but Nicklaus had perfected the charge; he was the most feared Sunday player in the game. He won his majors in virtually every way that you could win, but typically he won by coming from behind in the final round.

His last great challenger, of course, was Tom Watson. There is no need to reprise here their classic encounters; their duel in the 1977 British Open at Turnberry is one of the most illustrious pages in the history of championship golf. It marked yet another change in the perception of Nicklaus, the moment when he became the venerable old champion, and the moment when he became the underdog. After Turnberry, the odds were never overwhelmingly in his favor, and you could root enthusiastically for this stoic athlete who never stopped giving his absolute best.

There were more major championships, notably at St. Andrew's in 1978 and Baltusrol in 1980. In his remarks after the 1986 Masters, Nicklaus mentioned both of them. The rousing cheers that had borne him along in those two tournaments were long overdue, and they were sweet to him—another hint, if it's needed, of just how much he must have felt the absence of popular acclaim. Those last majors were nothing less than public celebrations, when the still-formidable old warrior reminded everyone of his former prowess. By then golf fans had to suppose that any Nicklaus victory might be the last, and savored accordingly.

*   *   *

After Nicklaus's last hard loss to Watson, at Pebble Beach in 1982, it seemed that all that remained was a summing up of his career. He kept playing the majors, but now he had passed into the shadows both of legend and of corporate endeavor. There was no simple way to assess his impact on the game of golf. You could consult the record book, and marvel at what he'd done as a player—but what about the championship courses he'd designed? Or the tournament, the Memorial, he'd established, which had become a fixture on the tour? Or the instruction books he'd written, and the videotapes he'd made? He was far and away the most influential teacher in the game, and thousands of players, young and old, tried to fashion their swings according to the principles he laid down.

Still more elusive was the influence he exerted on younger professionals. His sportsmanship was a standard for them and went a long way toward explaining why golf remained a gentlemanly game while other sports, with ever-larger prizes at stake, were played with barbaric manners. His devotion to his family provided another model to emulate. By now all five of his children were growing up, and Nicklaus, despite the pressures of his schedule, was determined that he would be as much a part of their lives as his own father was of his. He made, and kept, a promise to his wife, Barbara, that he would never be away from home for more than two weeks at a time. If you knew anything at all about Nicklaus, you knew that he had a set of strong values and loyalties—and that he lived by them.

He kept on playing golf, less often now, and less well. For years he'd been trimming back his schedule, prompting the waggish remark that he was "a legend in his spare time." When he did enter a tournament, though, he came to play. He worked on his game like any young pro looking to earn his spurs, tinkering endlessly with his swing, trying out tips that might help him get back into the groove. In many ways he was in the same situation as those younger men, competing against golfers in the prime of their careers, struggling to make cuts and having to content himself with distant finishes that made only the fine print in the tournament reports.

For Nicklaus, this was a new experience. He'd started at the top, without an apprenticeship, but now he was one of the pack. The game that had once come so easily to him was becoming more and more difficult, and you could only wonder when he would finally give up the stubborn ambition that kept urging him on. Like the young pros, he must have admitted to himself that the best players were now a stroke or two better than he was and that he would have to play a dream round to win another championship. Years earlier he only had to play like Jack Nicklaus, but now he would have to play like Jack Nicklaus *used* to play.

This, of course, is the predicament of every golfer, not just pros. The shimmering possibility of a glorious round is always there, always alluring, always receding. Every fan could identify with the frustrations and disappointments that Nicklaus was going through, the fresh hopes and high resolutions that had to precede every round.

And so, when he began his great surge in the Fiftieth Masters, golfers everywhere recognized the emotions he was feeling. He was winning the Masters as every golfer has won it in his fantasies, by playing a string of magnificent shots in front of an ecstatic gallery. The golf wasn't mortal, but the man—the man who kept fighting back tears—was. At long last it was clear that Jack Nicklaus was playing the same game that all the rest of us play, and his victory was a great victory for golf.

# Epilogue:
# Another Masters

Nicklaus's triumph cast a glow over the 1986 season, over-shadowing the disputes and controversies that had threatened to push themselves to the forefront of professional golf. Nicklaus seemed to have ushered in a sort of Indian summer for the game, restoring a luster to the majors and reinstating the familiar order in the kingdom.

He didn't do this single-handedly, of course, but he was very much in evidence throughout the summer, continuing to play first-class golf and to make his presence felt. After an irksome first round of 77 at the U.S. Open—won by the steely-eyed, forty-three-year-old Raymond Floyd in another hugely popular victory that also illustrated exactly what makes the majors the majors—he was too far behind to have a real crack at the title, but he closed out the tournament with fine rounds of 67 and 68. At the Memorial, the tournament that most golf insiders refer to simply as "Jack's tournament," he staged yet another of his patented charges on the last nine holes; and he kept his name on the leader board throughout the PGA.

Wherever he played, he drew admiring crowds who were happy just to lay eyes on him. The week after the PGA, for instance, he showed up to get in a practice round for the International, a tournament played at Castle Pines just outside Denver. It was late in the day. A light rain was falling and the course was nearly deserted. Still, the word spread swiftly that

Nicklaus had made his appearance, and a gallery of a hundred or so followed him out to the practice range and onto the course. One man had his son on his shoulders, and he kept telling the boy, in a voice full of wonder, "That's Jack Nicklaus, the greatest golfer who ever lived. Remember this—you're seeing a legend." The little boy couldn't have been more than three years old, and he couldn't have been anything but puzzled—by the fact that his father kept him out until dark, trudging for miles through a fine drizzle.

The crowd slipped and slid on the wet grass, over the up-and-down course that Nicklaus had designed in a spectacular Rocky Mountain setting. As much at ease as if he were in his own backyard, Nicklaus signed scores of autographs and bantered with the spectators, laughing at some of his own results—"That's a broken-bat single," he said of one drive that traveled about 260 yards—and at the maintenance of the course, frequently asking someone in the crowd to tell him where his ball had finished. He put in a plug for his oversized putter, too. His company, MacGregor, had sold thousands of them since the Masters, and when he ran in a sweet 10-footer, he asked, "Can you believe that anyone is still using that funny-looking *little* putter?"

Nicklaus was doing three things at once—inspecting his handiwork, playing a serious practice round, and basking in the adulation of the crowd—and he was unmistakably enjoying himself. So, obviously, were the fans. There was a kind of intimacy as they gathered round Nicklaus on the tees, and people kept talking excitedly to each other, recalling various Nicklausian deeds and seeming to take a personal pride in them. "He's still the Bear," one man said, almost gloating, when Nicklaus belted out a big drive. "He's my man."

At the ninth tee there was another treat in store. Nicklaus ran into another latecomer, Greg Norman, and the two linked up to play the back nine in the gathering darkness. They had plenty to talk about. They had become fast friends, a friendship that lent a particular meaning to the events of the season. Whatever feats Nicklaus might yet accomplish, his glory days were surely behind him. Norman, even though the summer had already brought him about as much glory as any golfer could expect, wasn't looking backward. The world—the world of championship golf—was still before him.

At that moment in August of 1986, you could have found thousands of golf fans ready to swear they'd seen the future, and the future was Greg Norman. As much as Nicklaus, and some would say even more than Nicklaus, he had put his imprint on the 1986 season, winning the British Open and pulling off a feat that was supposed to be impossible by leading all four of the majors after the third round. It had been years since anyone spoke of the Grand Slam as a real possibility, but Norman—in a day and age when the common wisdom dictated that no single golfer could dominate—had completed the "Saturday Slam." Along the way he won two other American tournaments and a pot full of money, playing a brand of golf that defied belief. His British Open victory was built on a second-round 63, tying the Open record for a low round; but that 63 could easily have been a 61. Norman had stumbled on the last two holes, three-putting on the final green, but still . . . a *61*. A score like that sounded like a pipe dream, but Norman, like Nicklaus before him, was redefining what was possible in professional golf.

Norman's streak began at Augusta. That bogey on the last hole looked to many spectators like further evidence that the Shark was nothing more than a world-class choke artist. To Norman, though, it had exactly the opposite meaning. His four consecutive birdies had brought him to the final hole riding a wave of confidence. How could he not go for the fifth birdie, the big, bold shot? *All or nothing* was more than just a phrase to Norman, it was a battle cry; and he left Augusta with the assurance that he was prepared, at last, to compete for the biggest prizes in golf.

There is no better way to describe his success than to cite the record. In the weeks following the Masters, Norman placed second at the Heritage, won the Las Vegas Invitational—the richest purse on the American tour—by seven strokes, and won the Kemper Open in a playoff with Larry Mize. He tied for 10th at the Memorial and 12th at the U.S.

Open where, in the third round, a heckler puffed himself up and made a public announcement that Norman was a choker. Seconds later the brave heckler was looking straight into Norman's ice-blue eyes with only the gallery rope separating them. Norman invited him to meet afterward to settle the matter, but the heckler declined.

Norman, admittedly, had lost his aplomb, and he was flat during the final round, slipping to a 75; but no one shrugs off disappointments and springs back more quickly than Greg Norman. The next morning he rose before dawn to appear on a television show, and then he drove back to Long Island for an outing. He larked about the golf course, needling his playing partners and bashing the ball over hazards that looked a mile away, generally giving the impression that he did not feel one iota of remorse.

Next came a third-place finish at Atlanta, another second place at the Canadian Open (and another mind-boggling round, a 62). After that it was the victory at the British Open, and now Norman was surely entitled to slack off a bit—but he didn't. The highs didn't unsettle him any more than the lows. He came in fifth at the Western Open and seemed to have the PGA wrapped up after three days. On the fourth day, on the 72d hole, Bob Tway blasted out of a bunker and into the hole, and Norman was denied another major. He must have felt, Jack Nicklaus said, "as if he'd been hit over the head with a two-by-four."

Even that didn't put him off his game. He did miss the cut at the International—and made a joke of it, pretending to choke on the grip of his sand iron. In September he went on a binge that carried him to six consecutive victories in Europe and Australia, a string that had golf writers scurrying to find precedents. Back in 1945 Byron Nelson ran off eleven straight victories on the American tour, and Tom Watson posted eight wins on three continents in 1980. But the most important parallel might have been Arnold Palmer's season in 1960, a year when he won eight events, including the U.S. Open and the Masters. In the opinion of many followers of the game, that was the year when professional golf secured its place in Ameri-

can sport, although the significance of Palmer's showing became much clearer in retrospect. Similarly, it may well appear
in years to come that Norman's 1986 season marked the beginning of a new era, a time when the best golfers played what
amounted to a world tour. Langer, Ballesteros, and others had
blazed the trail, but Norman's progress called attention to just
what a high and handsome trail it was. Perhaps the time had
come to speak of golf not as a kingdom, but as an empire.

The 1986 season, then, had served to showcase two golfers, Nicklaus and Norman, the Golden Bear representing a
departing generation, the Great White Shark a generation to
come. Nicklaus had gone out of his way to express his respect
for Norman, and the congratulations that meant the most to
Norman after his British Open victory came from Nicklaus,
who had climbed a television stanchion to watch the younger
man close out his win. Norman had been the only golfer who
remained at Augusta to congratulate Nicklaus, and Nicklaus
was returning the compliment. One of the many things the
two men had in common was an instinct for sportsmanship
that went far deeper than mere appearance. Another was their
devotion to family; Norman, despite his playboy image, never
let an opportunity pass to praise his wife (asked at the 1987
Masters how he felt about being left out of the Champions
Dinner, he replied immediately, "I did have dinner with a
champion last night—my wife"). Partly at Nicklaus's urging,
Norman had bought land in West Palm Beach, where the two
men would be neighbors. They even bore a certain physical
resemblance, with Norman a sleeker, streamlined, updated
version of Nicklaus—Nicklaus as Madison Avenue might have
designed him for the 1980s.

As the 1987 season began, Norman let it be known that he
wanted to win the Masters. "Not a day passes that I don't think
about it," he said in the early spring. He wanted his first green
jacket, and he wanted to be helped into it by Jack Nicklaus.

While Norman was rising to the top spot in the world
rankings, the spot coveted by Seve Ballesteros, the Spaniard
was losing ground, falling to third. His season wasn't without

its successes—he won six tournaments in Europe, including four in a row before the British Open—but they didn't have much savor, not when compared to Norman's wins and especially his performance in the majors. Ballesteros had been able to do no better than a tie for 24th at the U.S. Open, and he missed the cut at the PGA. His best finish was a 6th at the British Open—a rather hollow 6th, for he had never been close to the lead and shot a 64 on the final day to come from deep in the pack. "I'm having trouble with my driving, my irons, and my putting," he said at Turnberry. "The only thing I can think of to work on is my head."

That was the tone of many of the Spaniard's remarks. He hinted often at a loss of confidence and just as often lashed out at the nearest and most convenient target for criticism. The feud with Beman flared up again at the British Open, where Beman was a contestant ("What has this man done for European golf?" asked Ballesteros), and again at the PGA, where Beman invited him to take part in the World Series of Golf. Ballesteros was having none of it. When a reporter suggested that Beman might be looking for a truce, Ballesteros replied angrily, "No! He is not looking for peace. He is looking for more fire."

As moody as Hamlet, Ballesteros was clearly trying to put the loss at Augusta behind him. He bristled whenever the subject came up—and it did come up, repeatedly. The press kept asking him what had gone wrong on that 4-iron he hit at the 15th, but there was no answer Ballesteros could make to that question, or to the larger question that stood just behind it. Every great golfer—from Harry Vardon to Arnold Palmer, from Ben Hogan to Tom Watson—has sooner or later thrown away an important championship with an awful shot. In most cases it happens sooner, early in a golfer's career, but it had never happened to Ballesteros. He had always seemed proof against the tension that made other golfers buckle, and he never admitted publicly that he had felt any pressure at all on the 15th. His standard explanation was that he hadn't been able to make up his mind whether to play a hard 5-iron or a soft 4-iron and, consequently, made a tentative swing with the

4-iron. Privately, though, he referred to that shot as "a bad miracle"—a revealing remark from one who had always trusted *destino*. Had the fates turned on him? A championship golfer can't afford such doubts, not if he wants to keep on winning. Ballesteros's confidence had always set him apart, but now he was talking—and playing—as if his confidence had been shaken.

His suspension ran its course, and in 1987, under a new ruling, he was eligible to make eight tournament appearances in the United States. He chose his early-season tournaments carefully, once again pointing toward the Masters. This spring there were no boasts and no predictions, nothing but an ominous determination in his manner and appearance that struck many onlookers as a kind of obsession. A year ago he'd put his pride on the line at Augusta, and this year he was going to try to redeem it.

While Norman and Ballesteros entered the 1987 Masters as strong favorites, neither of them made much headway in the first two days of play. The course was giving up absolutely nothing. Only one player, John Cook, broke 70 in the opening round; his 69 made him the sole leader. Tom Watson shot a 71 and predicted—correctly, as it turned out—that four rounds of 71, or four under par, would win the tournament. Curtis Strange moved to the front in the second round with a total of 141, a stroke ahead of Roger Maltbie, whose 66, under the conditions, was more like a magic act than a round of golf.

Once again the greens were a subject of frequent and exasperated conversation. This year they weren't only fast but firmer than ever. The bent grass had a bluish, shaven look, and balls made a hissing sound when they pitched onto the greens, a noise like a zipper closing. They took several bounces before they settled down. To the pros, used to making their approach shots check up sharply, this was a different game, and it was made even more difficult by the fact that the grass in the fairways was slightly higher than usual, just high enough to make a ball sit down in it—and the golfers couldn't always get all of the ball on the clubface. "It's like hitting out of a hayfield onto a highway," one pro said, and added, "It's work out there." Larry Mize, a native of Augusta and a sentimental favorite who managed to stay close to the lead, looked drawn and weary when he came off the course after his second round. He'd shot a 72, but he said, "I feel like I just played thirty-six holes, not eighteen."

On Saturday Norman strapped on his seven-league boots. He had to; he'd shot 73–74 in the opening rounds, and there were twenty-four golfers ahead of him. With a round of 66, he overtook all but two of them. His three-round total was 213, and one streak had ended—he wasn't in the lead at the end of play on Saturday but a stroke behind Maltbie and Ben Crenshaw, who had also made a giant step: he brought in a 67.

Ballesteros was at 214, but his scores had improved day by day: 73–71–70. As always, he was able to communicate his emotions to the gallery, but the emotion he communicated most powerfully was torment. It was almost painful to watch him play (months after the tournament, looking at photographs of himself in action, Ballesteros remarked, "Somewhere out there I lost my youth"). In golf there is such a thing as trying too hard, and Ballesteros looked as if he might be guilty of it.

Still, he was in touch with the leaders when the final day began, a Sunday when there was a grim and general falling away. The play followed the same inexorable pattern established in the first three days. There were eight men within two strokes of the lead, and six of them would hold or share it before the day was through. But this was a championship of attrition.

Only three contenders were able to play the front nine in better than par. One of them, Larry Mize, put together a 35 made up of three birdies and two bogeys. Jodie Mudd bolted out to a sensational start, opening birdie, eagle, birdie. In fact, the loudest cheer of the morning came from the gallery at the second green when Mudd's perfectly cut 3-wood split the bunkers at the front of the green and curled toward the flag. It seemed to have double eagle written all over it . . . but only burned the cup. When Mudd added the birdie at No. 3, he was four under par for the round, three under for the tournament; and as the fortunes of the other contenders waxed and waned, that was looking like the score to beat.

The third man who rallied on the front nine was Jack Nicklaus. With birdies on the two par 5s, he made the turn in 34 and got to one under par, but not even Nicklaus could pry any strokes out of the back nine. With bogeys at No. 10 and No. 11 and an eagle at No. 13—"the only putt I made all week," Nicklaus said—he finished with a 70. In the last round of a major, the Golden Bear could still gather himself for a roar.

Ballesteros had one birdie and one bogey on the front nine. The bogey came at the short 6th, where he nearly four-putted. He'd been handling the greens about as well as anyone, but his second putt on this green, a four-footer, rimmed the cup and picked up speed as it switched out. The putt coming back was every bit as long as the one he had just missed, and Ballesteros looked stricken. Somehow he pulled himself together to save his bogey, but it was hard to see how he could keep putting so much pressure on himself and stay among the leaders. He did make a birdie at the 9th, but dropped back to one under with a bogey at the 11th. With birdies few and far between, his chances were slipping away. Through 63 holes, Ballesteros posted only nine birdies—and in 1983 he had set a Masters record with 23.

Norman, too, was barely hanging on. His front nine was up-and-down, with three bogeys and two birdies. He should have scored a third birdie at No. 9, where he slammed his drive all the way to the foot of the hill and swallowed up the flag with a wedge. But then he missed the four-footer and his putter went cold. At the 10th his putt to save par hung on the lip, and he three-putted No. 11 for another bogey. Now he stood at even par for the tournament, facing the same task he'd faced a year ago. He was going to have to reel off a string of birdies.

Ben Crenshaw, holding steady at three under, was looking more and more like the man to beat. Mudd had fallen back to two under, and Crenshaw had negotiated Amen Corner without losing a stroke. He was in the fringe on several holes, but his chipping was crisp and his putter was holding up under the

strain. On the 12th, and again on the 14th, he coaxed in delicate, lengthy putts to save pars. When he lifted his ball from
the cup at No. 16, he had posted nine pars in a row. Two more
and he was home with at least a share of the lead.

At about the same time, Larry Mize was walking up the
last fairway. He'd hit a good drive, but at two under, he had
to have a birdie on the finishing hole; he'd followed back-to-
back birdies at No. 12 and No. 13 with back-to-back bogeys on
the next two holes. The golfer who everyone said was almost
too nice, the golfer who had crumbled in other tournaments,
this same golfer, Larry Mize, came through with a courageous,
championship shot. From 140 yards out he hit a full-blooded
9-iron to the green. The pin was cut in its traditional position
on the lower terrace. The ball pitched onto the green not more
than three feet from the cup, skipped, started up the incline—
and then looped back down to finish pin-high, six feet from the
hole. Mize hit the putt as if he meant it, and the ball was in the
center of the cup. At three under, he was the surprising new
leader.

As soon as Mize stepped off the green, Ballesteros appeared in the last fairway. At the same time, a red 3 went into
the slot beside his name on the scoreboard, showing that he
had birdied the 17th. His other birdie on the back nine must
have been especially gratifying, for it came at the 15th. As a
matter of fact, Ballesteros had nearly made it three birdies in
a row; his 12-footer at No. 16 hung shimmering on the lip of
the cup.

Like Mize, though, he had done what was necessary. Another birdie now would give him the lead outright, but he
pushed his approach shot and watched it splash down in the
bunker. After four days of implacable pursuit, this Masters
could still get away from him, and to lose again, on the last hole
. . . no golfer deserved that kind of punishment. The ball
floated up, out of the sand, settled down softly on the green,
and Ballesteros made the same putt Mize had just made.

Now there were two players tied for the lead, and Greg
Norman came striding up the last fairway. Actually, he came
striding through it, veering to the left to follow the path of his

tee shot. It had flown the fairway bunkers at the turn of the dogleg—bunkers that were put there expressly to stop a young powerhouse named Jack Nicklaus from ignoring the dogleg and attacking this green from the rough. No one could remember any golfer who had cleared them. And while the marshals were trying to get rid of a green litter bag near Norman's ball, the red 3 showed up on the scoreboard beside his name.

Shades of 1986! Then, too, Norman had come to the final hole needing a par to tie and a birdie to win. Then, too, he had played into an area normally occupied by the gallery. Then, too, he had collected four birdies on the back nine—and this year, if he hadn't also bogeyed No. 16, he would have come to the finishing hole needing only a par to win.

With a bunker to carry, and the pin tucked behind the bunker, he hit about the best shot anyone could have hit, a high wedge that stayed on the lower terrace of the green. Without any fuss, he lined up the 20-foot putt and sent it on its excruciating course. His caddy, who has a theatrical habit of leaving the flagstick in the hole until the last possible instant, leaned over to look the ball into the cup. He was sure that it was in. The entire gallery, which now included a majority of those on the course, started to rumble. Ballesteros and Mize, watching on television in the Bob Jones Cabin—where Nicklaus had watched Norman a year ago—thought the ball had a chance. Norman *knew* he'd made the putt and crouched, ready to spring into the air, ready for "the whole place to erupt." When the ball was a foot from the hole, the caddy at last pulled the flag to let it fall—and somehow, it stayed out.

The gallery was still muttering as the last pairing of the day came into view. The Masters has a tradition of producing tense finishes, but this was ridiculous: Both Crenshaw and Maltbie were at two under, and if they birdied the last hole, five golfers would go to the 10th tee for a playoff.

The key hole for Crenshaw and Maltbie had been the 17th. Maltbie, who'd scotched his prospects with a series of feeble chip shots, had birdied the hole; and Crenshaw, who'd been so steady, had finally missed a putt and bogeyed it. Now both of them had a crack at more or less the same putt that

Norman had just missed; they both missed, and a three-man playoff it would be.

There was no time to reflect on the game way that Maltbie had battled back or the hard loss that Crenshaw had endured. Norman, Ballesteros, and Mize were already loosening up on the 10th tee, preparing for the third sudden-death playoff in Masters history, and this one had the makings of a classic. It was, after all, the confrontation that most people had expected at the beginning of the tournament, though it was a long and tortuous 72 holes in the making.

Mize, a much slighter man than either of the other two, didn't seem to stand much of a chance. He had won only one professional tournament, the 1983 Memphis Classic, and he had faltered badly in two others he might have won. At the 1986 Kemper Open, he had three-putted on the final green to let Norman into a playoff, and that same year he lost a comfortable lead over the closing holes of the Tournament Players Championship. He'd earned a reputation as a weak finisher, but he gave the hometown crowd something to cheer about when he outdrove Ballesteros and Norman by a good 40 yards. Then, when they both flew their iron shots onto the back of the 10th green, he hit a pretty 7-iron that finished well inside them, 12 feet from the hole and below it.

Ballesteros was the first to putt. He took his time lining up his ball, and the gallery marshals had to move back the crowd. Now, in late afternoon, the sun was coming in low, and the shadows of the gallery fell close to Ballesteros's ball. Finally, when all was quiet and still, Ballesteros ran his ball boldly at the cup, too boldly. The ball ghosted a good five feet past. Norman and Mize both missed, too, and Ballesteros went to work on the kind of grisly par-saver he'd been making throughout the tournament.

The ball never touched the cup, and another Masters was over for Ballesteros. Dazed, uncertain whether to pick up his ball or hole out, Ballesteros waited on the green until Mize and Norman had holed out, then shook hands and began the long trek back up the 10th fairway. It had to be the most desolate walk he ever made on a golf course, and it must have felt as if he'd been exiled. Tears streamed down his face every step of the way.

Norman and Mize moved on. They both hit good drives at No. 11, but Mize was away. This time, though, his approach sailed wide to the right, and he turned his back in disgust. He'd given Norman an opening. Choosing not to flirt with the flag and the pond guarding it, Norman played safely to the right edge of the green. From there he was confident he could get down in two.

The pressure was all on Mize now. His ball was a full twenty paces from the edge of the green, which sloped away from him toward the pond. A touch strong, and he would run his ball way past the hole. On the other hand, a weak shot would lose its pace in the fringe and finish short, leaving him a downhill putt. Either way, he would be looking at an almost certain bogey.

He made the only choice he could make, to chip the ball firmly. It hopped twice in the fringe and ran toward the cup. Standing at the bottom of the green, watching from the side, Norman judged from the speed of the ball that it would be five or six feet past the hole. He couldn't see the line—but Mize could, and so could the huge gallery that was pressed against the ropes in Amen Corner. The ball was dead on the stick. It never swerved. When it hit the pin and vanished, Larry Mize threw his wedge aside and leapt high into the air as if he had cleared a huge hurdle.

For Norman, who missed his long putt, the 1987 Masters was the bitterest loss of all, as it had been for Ballesteros. Yet the tournament completed a cycle, ending the drama that had begun the year before. Larry Mize had wiped the slate clean.

A new season was under way. Neither Norman nor Ballesteros had the sort of year expected of them, but Norman could hardly have matched his performance of 1986, and Ballesteros, who won only one tournament in Europe, had his shining hours in the Ryder Cup matches at the end of the season. For the first time in history, the European team won on American soil—and they won at Muirfield Village, on a course designed by Jack Nicklaus, against a team captained by him.

The Ryder Cup produced marvelous golf, and it provided another glimpse into the future, that same future that Greg Norman had illuminated in 1986. To put it simply, the sport had outgrown the confines of any single national organization. There were good golfers to be found all over the globe, and Jack Nicklaus broke the news to all who cared to listen. "Golf has become a world sport," he said, "and we shouldn't try to stand in its way. We should try to help it."

Out with the old, and in with the new! It was typical of Nicklaus to look forward so staunchly even though a new generation could get along perfectly well without him. As well as anyone can, he understands that the game has a life and mind of its own, that it is larger than any single player. In golf's global future, it will surely be more difficult for any player, including Norman and Ballesteros, to make the kind of mark that Nicklaus made. When the history of the game comes to be written, a whole era will bear his name, and its last and most luminous page will be the story of the 1986 Masters.

# Appendix:
# Final Standings

# FINAL STANDINGS

| PLAYER<br>*First 24 Finishers and ties:* | | SCORE | | | | TOTAL | PRIZE<br>MONEY |
|---|---|---|---|---|---|---|---|
| Jack Nicklaus | 1 | 74 | 71 | 69 | 65 | 279 | $144,000 |
| Tom Kite | T-2 | 70 | 74 | 68 | 68 | 280 | 70,400 |
| Greg Norman (Australia) | T-2 | 70 | 72 | 68 | 70 | 280 | 70,400 |
| Severiano Ballesteros (Spain) | 4 | 71 | 68 | 72 | 70 | 281 | 38,400 |
| Nick Price (Zimbabwe) | 5 | 79 | 69 | 63 | 71 | 282 | 32,000 |
| Jay Haas | T-6 | 76 | 69 | 71 | 67 | 283 | 27,800 |
| Tom Watson | T-6 | 70 | 74 | 68 | 71 | 283 | 27,800 |
| Tsuneyuki Nakajima (Japan) | T-8 | 70 | 71 | 71 | 72 | 284 | 23,200 |
| Payne Stewart | T-8 | 75 | 71 | 69 | 69 | 284 | 23,200 |
| Bob Tway | T-8 | 70 | 73 | 71 | 70 | 284 | 23,200 |
| Donnie Hammond | T-11 | 73 | 71 | 67 | 74 | 285 | 16,960 |
| Sandy Lyle (Scotland) | T-11 | 76 | 70 | 68 | 71 | 285 | 16,960 |
| Mark McCumber | T-11 | 76 | 67 | 71 | 71 | 285 | 16,960 |
| Corey Pavin | T-11 | 71 | 72 | 71 | 71 | 285 | 16,960 |
| Calvin Peete | T-11 | 75 | 71 | 69 | 70 | 285 | 16,960 |
| Dave Barr (Canada) | T-16 | 70 | 77 | 71 | 68 | 286 | 12,000 |
| Ben Crenshaw | T-16 | 71 | 71 | 74 | 70 | 286 | 12,000 |
| Gary Koch | T-16 | 69 | 74 | 71 | 72 | 286 | 12,000 |
| Bernhard Langer (West Germany) | T-16 | 74 | 68 | 69 | 75 | 286 | 12,000 |
| Larry Mize | T-16 | 75 | 74 | 72 | 65 | 286 | 12,000 |
| Curtis Strange | T-21 | 73 | 74 | 68 | 72 | 287 | 9,300 |
| Fuzzy Zoeller | T-21 | 73 | 73 | 69 | 72 | 287 | 9,300 |
| Tze-Chung Chen (Republic of China) | T-23 | 69 | 73 | 75 | 71 | 288 | 8,000 |
| Roger Maltbie | T-23 | 71 | 75 | 69 | 73 | 288 | 8,000 |

| PLAYER<br>*Remaining Players Who Completed 72 Holes:* | | SCORE | | | | TOTAL | PRIZE<br>MONEY |
|---|---|---|---|---|---|---|---|
| Bill Glasson | T-25 | 72 | 74 | 72 | 71 | 289 | 6,533 |
| Peter Jacobsen | T-25 | 75 | 73 | 68 | 73 | 289 | 6,533 |
| Scott Simpson | T-25 | 76 | 72 | 67 | 74 | 289 | 6,533 |
| Danny Edwards | T-28 | 71 | 71 | 72 | 76 | 290 | 5,667 |
| David Graham (Australia) | T-28 | 76 | 72 | 74 | 68 | 290 | 5,667 |
| Johnny Miller | T-28 | 74 | 70 | 77 | 69 | 290 | 5,667 |
| Fred Couples | T-31 | 72 | 77 | 70 | 72 | 291 | 4,875 |
| Bruce Lietzke | T-31 | 78 | 70 | 68 | 75 | 291 | 4,875 |
| Dan Pohl | T-31 | 76 | 70 | 72 | 73 | 291 | 4,875 |
| Lanny Wadkins | T-31 | 78 | 71 | 73 | 69 | 291 | 4,875 |
| Wayne Levi | 35 | 73 | 76 | 67 | 76 | 292 | 4,300 |
| Rick Fehr | T-36 | 75 | 74 | 69 | 75 | 293 | 3,850 |
| Hubert Green | T-36 | 71 | 75 | 73 | 74 | 293 | 3,850 |
| Larry Nelson | T-36 | 73 | 73 | 71 | 76 | 293 | 3,850 |
| Sam W. Randolph | T-36 | 75 | 73 | 72 | 73 | 293 | Amateur |
| Tony Sills | T-36 | 76 | 73 | 73 | 71 | 293 | 3,850 |
| Don Pooley | 41 | 77 | 72 | 73 | 72 | 294 | 3,400 |
| Bill Kratzert | T-42 | 68 | 72 | 76 | 79 | 295 | 3,200 |
| John Mahaffey | T-42 | 79 | 69 | 72 | 75 | 295 | 3,200 |
| Ken Green | 44 | 68 | 78 | 74 | 76 | 296 | 3,000 |
| Phil Blackmar | T-45 | 76 | 73 | 73 | 76 | 298 | 2,700 |
| Jim Thorpe | T-45 | 74 | 74 | 73 | 77 | 298 | 2,700 |
| Lee Trevino | 47 | 76 | 73 | 73 | 77 | 299 | 2,500 |
| Mark O'Meara | 48 | 74 | 73 | 81 | 73 | 301 | 2,300 |

| PLAYER<br>*Players Who Did Not Make the Cut-Off (149):* | SCORE | | TOTAL | PRIZE<br>MONEY |
|---|---|---|---|---|
| Gary Player (South Africa) | 77 | 73 | 150 | 1,500 |
| Craig Stadler | 74 | 76 | 150 | 1,500 |
| Andy Bean | 75 | 76 | 151 | 1,500 |
| Bob Eastwood | 79 | 72 | 151 | 1,500 |
| Buddy Gardner | 74 | 77 | 151 | 1,500 |
| Gary Hallberg | 78 | 73 | 151 | 1,500 |
| Kenny Knox | 75 | 76 | 151 | 1,500 |
| George Burns | 74 | 78 | 152 | 1,500 |
| Ray Floyd | 74 | 78 | 152 | 1,500 |
| Dan Forsman | 78 | 74 | 152 | 1,500 |
| Hale Irwin | 76 | 76 | 152 | 1,500 |
| Robert C. Lewis, Jr. | 74 | 78 | 152 | Amateur |
| Mac O'Grady | 82 | 70 | 152 | 1,500 |
| R. Jay Sigel | 74 | 78 | 152 | Amateur |
| Joey Sindelar | 79 | 73 | 152 | 1,500 |
| Hal Sutton | 80 | 72 | 152 | 1,500 |
| Gay Brewer, Jr. | 77 | 76 | 153 | 1,500 |
| Billy Casper | 78 | 75 | 153 | 1,500 |
| Charles Coody | 76 | 77 | 153 | 1,500 |
| Chip Drury | 76 | 77 | 153 | Amateur |
| Peter Persons | 76 | 77 | 153 | Amateur |
| Jack Renner | 76 | 77 | 153 | 1,500 |
| Jack Kay, Jr. (Canada) | 80 | 74 | 154 | Amateur |
| Larry Rinker | 73 | 81 | 154 | 1,500 |
| Doug Tewell | 74 | 80 | 154 | 1,500 |
| Scott R. Verplank | 77 | 77 | 154 | Amateur |
| Mark Wiebe | 76 | 78 | 154 | 1,500 |
| George Archer | 75 | 80 | 155 | 1,500 |
| Tommy Aaron | 79 | 77 | 156 | 1,500 |
| Isao Aoki (Japan) | 79 | 77 | 156 | 1,500 |
| Doug Ford | 78 | 78 | 156 | 1,500 |
| Garth M. McGimpsey (Northern Ireland) | 78 | 78 | 156 | Amateur |
| Arnold Palmer | 80 | 76 | 156 | 1,500 |
| Michael E. Podolak | 82 | 74 | 156 | Amateur |
| Bill Rogers | 80 | 76 | 156 | 1,500 |
| Denis Watson (South Africa) | 80 | 76 | 156 | 1,500 |
| Tim Simpson | 78 | 79 | 157 | 1,500 |
| Randy Sonnier | 81 | 77 | 158 | Amateur |
| Tze-Ming Chen (Republic of China) | 79 | 81 | 160 | 1,500 |
| Bob Goalby | 79 | 81 | 160 | 1,500 |
| | | TOTAL | | $805,100 |